Alan Jamieson is a minister who has also trained as a sociologist. His PhD, on which his book *A Churchless Faith* (SPCK, 2002) is based, researched why people leave their churches and their continuing journeys of faith outside the Church. From this study, he and others at Wellington Central Baptist Church, New Zealand, have formed groups and networks with people who are traversing difficult phases of faith and exploring new horizons beyond the present structures of 'church'. Alan is a research associate of the Tyndale Graduate School of Theology.

Journeying in Faith

In and Beyond the Tough Places

ALAN JAMIESON

First published in Great Britain in 2004 by
Society for Promoting Christian Knowledge
Holy Trinity Church
Marylebone Road
London NW1 4DU

British Library Cataloguing-in-Publication Data
A catalogue record for this book is available from the British Library

ISBN 0-281-05589-0

1 3 5 7 9 10 8 6 4 2

Designed and typeset by Kenneth Burnley, Wirral, Cheshire
Printed in Great Britain by Antony Rowe, Chippenham, Wiltshire

Contents

Preface

————◀◦▶————

Not all who wander are lost.
(J. R. R. Tolkien)[1]

The pages that follow are for faith wanderers who sometimes feel
lost or whom others would describe as lost. They are for those who
find themselves inextricably drawn beyond the confines of institutional 'churchianity' toward unknown horizons of Christian faith.
The book began as personal musings on the issues facing postmodern, post-christendom Christians, turned into a series of talks
that Rodney Macann, Jenny McIntosh and I worked on together,
and then with many changes and alterations became this story – a
story which is a composite of many people's journeys that I have
had the privilege of being able to collect, consider and re-tell.
I hope in our stories you will find hope in your own difficult
wanderings of faith.

In putting this book together I need to thank all those whose
journeys are reflected directly and indirectly here. Thank you, too,
to the people of Central, the faith community in which I belong,
for your love and support both to me and to many other wanderers
who are trying to make sense of faith and life in our wilderness
times of new horizons. I am indebted to the team of great people I
work with for their friendship and support – thank you Jenny,
Rodney, Sally, Delwyn and Zena; especially to Jenny McIntosh for
her feedback, comments and thoughts as this book has developed,
and for being open to journey with people in the difficult places of
faith. Jenny facilitates a number of small groups, resources for
groups and a regular newsletter for people outside church structures under the umbrella of 'Spirited Exchanges'.

Although we live in a somewhat bewildering time which poses many new challenges and threats for followers of Christ, we are also privileged to live in an age where modern communication allows us to connect so easily with each other. I very much appreciate hearing from people, learning from their stories and finding out what works for them and what does not. If you would like to make contact, or know more about 'Spirited Exchanges', my e-mail address is aj@paradise.net.nz.

1

Finding Our Way

————◆◇◆————

Blessed are those whose strength is in you,
who have set their hearts on pilgrimage.[1]

Mark Yeah, that's my observation, people do get stuck and a lot of
people get stuck in their faith. Most don't confront the faith crises
and tend to go with the flow too much. They tend not to have the
ability, the resources or the human contact to actually face the
challenge and work through it. That is one thing that I have noticed,
there is a huge gap when it comes to 'being there' for people.

Over the last seven years since Mark said these words he has
moved on from the crisis of faith in which he was immersed. For
him a way of making sense of his faith crisis and friends, including
'one or two non-Christians and a small group of others' immersed
in a similar faith struggle, has helped him move through a very
dark and lonely period in his Christian faith – a period in which he
left the church he had been a part of and highly committed to for
many years. This church had encouraged him as he completed his
theological degree and is still the church where a number of his key
friends continued to be involved. Yet despite these strong ties he
couldn't stay in that kind of environment and he couldn't continue
to attend the services the church was offering as he traversed his
dark night of the soul.

This book is for people like Mark and those willing to
accompany others like him. However, before jumping in and
talking about the book, we need to tease out Mark's story a little
more.

Mark's first introduction to Christians was through friends who
were trying to convert him. Despite their enthusiastic efforts he

wasn't going to be dragged into a faith he wasn't interested in. He remembers vividly being at a party while in his late teens; he'd drunk too much and had a woman sitting on his knee.

> *Mark* I couldn't remember who she was; this was before I became a Christian. I was around 18 or 19, and we were talking about Christianity and religion. I remember asking her what she thought about it all. Even in those days I was quite aware and wanted to talk about it with people. I remember saying to her, one day I'm going to become a Christian but not yet.

Not long after this party a personal crisis overcame Mark's reluctance to let God interfere with his lifestyle and he went along with his friends to a service at a local Pentecostal church. While some of the things they did appeared 'pretty weird' it also struck him 'that they were genuinely quite impressive people in their own right and they certainly had something that was worth considering'. Mark became a Christian. He was 20 years old. From day one he was 'full-on', and 'heavily involved'. He describes it saying, 'At that time it was pretty much full-on commitment. You know you smoked it, breathed it, twice on Sundays. I was involved in the youth group, leading or running the youth group, going to a home group, all that sort of stuff – right into it.'

Later, because of church leadership struggles and a growing number of friends at another church, he made the move from the Pentecostal church which he had been actively involved in for the previous five or six years to a large charismatic mainline[2] church. It was through this church that he became involved in a group caring for ex-psychiatric patients who were moving out of residential care and into the community. For Mark this meant time dealing with severely depressed people, and people who were reacting badly to medication or who had withdrawn themselves from regular medication. Many of these people had been institutionalized for long periods and were now struggling to make their way in wider society. At times Mark was involved in working with people who were threatening to take their own lives or were suffering from delusions of grandeur or evil. A formative part of this work was a friendship he built with a paranoid schizophrenic. Dealing with his friend and others in the group raised a lot of questions for Mark about his faith. 'Does God heal schizophrenia?

You know, all those really good ones', he told me with a quizzical smile on his face. For Mark, this was not some academic or distant question, but one of a cluster of pressing personal issues that were beginning to confront him. While Mark was a key leader in the ministry to ex-psychiatric patients, he was also an active member of one of the church home groups, a number of church outreaches and the church evangelism programme.

> *Mark* I was involved in trying to do evangelism in our area . . . sort of a door-to-door thing. So we went around with these surveys; when I think of it now it was just a foot in the door. We were doing a survey, but really we wanted to talk about God.

Perhaps because of the faith questions, especially those raised through his leadership of the psychiatric group more than any other single reason, Mark enrolled to spend three years at a theological college studying for a bachelor's degree in theology. For Mark, this was a stimulating faith environment.

> *Mark* Parts of it I thoroughly, absolutely enjoyed. I loved the contradiction. We did biblical formal, source criticism, redaction criticism and all that stuff. People were just about throwing their faith away, and I was just lapping it up. This stuff made sense, the whole idea of the different sources and having a different perspective, not being synthesized and all the 'jots and tittles' weren't exactly the same. Rather they were all from different points of view. Yeah, I liked the fact that all kinds of things were being knocked over and re-formed. Preconceptions, all of these amazing delicious new ideas. You know, I love new ideas. So that part of it I really thoroughly enjoyed.

When Mark returned to his home church complete with a degree, he was struck by the question of what he should do now. The church seemed to have high expectations of him, and so did he, but these were being radically undermined by a period of personal confusion and despair. As he says, 'As best as I can fathom, basically I think I got depressed . . . all the classic depression signs, waking up early in the morning, not sleeping, not enjoying anything . . .' Throughout this period he felt he was not meeting either his own or the church's expectations of him.

Mark You build an amazing amount of self-expectation after doing three years at theological college. And even before that, the whole Christian emphasis is on doing and being; doing things for God and being a particular kind of person. When you don't meet up to your own expectations of what a Christian should do and be, a crisis takes place. Suddenly you almost feel powerless to do and be what you should do and be, and you go to church. I went and I would hear all these messages about what I should do and be. And the word 'should' is probably something that still rings in my ears now. Something that characterizes church is the word 'should'.

This led to feelings of guilt and a sense of failure. At times Mark said he felt quite selfish and self-centred and was only dragging himself around. He tried to explain 'where he was at' to one of the leaders of the church:

Mark I remember trying to tell a guy at church once how I was feeling. He just went sort of cold turkey. He couldn't deal with it. He was a guy who you would say was a mature person, but he just couldn't deal with it. Another day he asked me if he could pray with me and I told him no (ha ha). I thought, you can't even listen to me, you haven't even earned the right. Maybe the word 'earned' is a bit harsh, but that was how I felt.

Over a period of months Mark drifted out of this church and had a period of six months completely outside of any church participation before spasmodically attending a mainstream liturgical church in the back row. During his six-month break from church he took a course of mild anti-depressants, went to counselling and joined a group of questioners like himself who had been brought together by a Christian psychotherapist.

It was at this point that I interviewed Mark as part of a socio-logical study of the faith journeys of adult Christians who left evangelical, Pentecostal and charismatic churches (EPC). The results of this study and Mark's story can be found in *A Church-less Faith*.[3] Recently I went back to the participants and asked how their faith had changed during the intervening years. For Mark it had been seven years since I had sat down and listened to his story. Now he is in a quite different place in terms of his faith and church connections from where he was when we first talked. He describes

4

himself as 'having a re-discovery of the beauty and power of grace and a growing confidence in his Christian faith'. He is part of an exploratory church in which there are a number of people traversing similar ground to Mark, where he feels he belongs and finds the expressions of faith 'frank, funny, real and tragic'. Describing his faith he says:

> *Mark* My faith is inseparable from me. My experience gives integrity to my faith.

Speaking of his beliefs he says, 'They are more fluid now' and he has little interest in great theories. What he looks for now is a grounded and practical faith. Mark continues to have personal experiences of God through music, his friendships, nature and his church community. Prayer has become more focused on 'relationship building . . . a sense of one-ness with God, being transported to another space. It is a remembering of who I am and who God is.' But for Mark, prayer is now less about 'changing events'. He says, 'I am very reticent to ask for anything now.' After putting the Bible down for a long time and not referring to it or reading it, he says he is 'slowly opening it again'. At times he finds the 'language very harsh' but he's sure of its significance despite his difficulties in understanding it. He talks about moving back into forms of community action and service as an outworking of his Christian faith, and although not keen on the word 'mission', because of many of its connotations, he is relaxed when it comes to talking about his beliefs and the result of his faith in his own life.

Many people like Mark are traversing very difficult, often lonely and dark places of faith: places that we naturally run from, places on the Christian journey that many come up against but few journey through. In such places, resources like those Mark found – friendships, a small group of fellow-wanderers and the accounts of those who have journeyed through similarly desperate places – can be incredibly helpful and hopeful.

This book sets out to tell some of these stories, to encourage connections with people who know about the difficulty of these dark places of faith, and to provide some resources that may be useful. In order to protect people's confidentiality the names used are fictional but the comments are direct quotes from real people's journeys. Each name has only been allocated once so readers can trace the comments of each person throughout this book.

Before we move on there are two other significant groups of people for whom this book is intended, for it is not just the church leavers that we need to listen to, although clearly in their absence from institutional forms of church they are capturing the attention of many researchers and church leaders. We need also to listen to the churchless faith of people who never leave a church. Recently I spent an evening with a group of middle-aged adults who were all part of churches in their neighbouring district. They were, in fact, a 'Who's Who' of church leaderships and would have been seen by any minister as significant players in the life of their respective churches and the local community. These were people who were obviously intelligent, theologically literate, long-term committed Christians. They had been meeting together for a number of months because they were all struggling with their continued connection with their churches. To be honest, most were just hanging on to the edge of their respective churches. Often bored and completely uninvolved with the services and other activities, they nevertheless regularly attended. I'm sure this group is being multiplied all over the Western world as thousands of similar people meet over lunches in cafés, over a beer in the local pub or in homes to talk about their feelings that they no longer seem to fit in the very church community they once greatly valued. This is a trend to which we cannot close our eyes.

The title 'churchless faith' belongs to these internal leavers as much as those who physically leave, never to come back. The title fits because their faith is not presently being supported, encouraged or developed by their church. If circumstances were different they would probably leave altogether, but they tend to have their own valid reasons for continuing their church attendance and involvement long after church has become unhelpful, maybe even damaging to their own faith experience. Some have children or teenagers whom they want to see grounded in the church community and Christian faith. For some, their spouse is still keenly involved. Some have close friendships, responsibilities or activities within the wider Church that remain significant to them. Some need to be connected to a church because of their work, and some simply like the music. Others stay on because they see no other viable alternative. I have met hundreds of them, and suggest there are probably some in every church community. While they may not be there every week, they are around often enough to seem like regulars. Most have long since given away the idea of talking about how they feel, or about their questions, doubts or irritations. They have either seen the glazed look of disbelief on the part of church leaders or watched as others who asked questions or complained were sidelined. They may also realize, from what is said at the front of the church, that this isn't a place for their concerns and feelings of discontent. We need to remember that while much is being said about church leavers (those who vacate the pews and are no longer to be found in church services, home groups, mission groups, evangelistic programmes or on the church address list) they are not the only church leavers. We must also remember those who are physically involved in one or more, maybe all, of the activities of their respective church communities and yet have left internally. Physically they still take up spaces on the pews and appear on the church attendance graphs, but deep inside the 'lights are off' and they may well have been off for some time. These internal leavers are the ones Mary Tuomi Hammond, an American pastor who does much work with church leavers, has said 'are one step from the door'.

> They feel that their concerns do not mirror those of their faith community: their questions are not taken seriously, their histories are unsafe to share, their passion for ministry goes unsupported. They struggle to remain faithful to the church, secretly they ask themselves 'Why am I in this place? Why should I stay?'[4]

These are the feelings Jamie described about his own internal leaving:

Jamie For me it's the sort of experiential stuff of going to church, being involved in the church and feeling that it is entirely unrewarding, irrelevant. I'd heard it before. The same old concepts trotted out. I don't know – it had lost its meaning. It didn't seem to be connected to anything in my life that I felt was important. And I was aware that I was increasingly reacting negatively to things . . . I guess it was an increasing realization that I just didn't like or enjoy the people that I was associated with in church. I felt like I didn't have much in common with them. I didn't respect them.

Put simply, the following five criteria describe their experiences. Though these internal leavers have not physically left, they have a growing sense of:

- *Disenchantment* – they do not enjoy church any more because it no longer fascinates or interests them. This disenchantment can lead to a critical view of all they once enjoyed and endorsed as they become its judge, losing any sense of loyalty they may have had as they no longer feel associated with their (or any) church in the same way.
- *Disillusionment* – for differing reasons they feel let down, sad, perhaps cynical, and often quite destructive in their view of the church. What was once life-giving now feels lifeless, and they can wonder if, after all, they are wasting their time. With disillusionment comes a disengagement from the church.
- *Disengagement* – they feel they are no longer connected, interested or involved in what is going on in the church structures, direction and community.
- *Disidentification* – they no longer identify with the church, the activities, worship and people there, and begin to observe as an outsider would.
- *Disorientation* – they don't know where they belong any more. This is often coupled with a sense of having lost their bearings, their anchor, perhaps even their identity. Sometimes the sense of disorientation is linked to feelings of loss and uncertainty and, with it, a new anxiety can creep in. Typically this is also linked to a sense of freedom, curiosity about the future, and excitement about possibilities ahead.

As Jamie said:

> *Jamie* You know there was this feeling within me that the people I do like and respect are these other people outside of the church. That was quite an influence on me – a sense of coming to my senses and saying 'What am I doing, what is the point of this? There didn't appear to be any impact on my life.'

This book then is written for the Jamies and the Marks, those who physically leave their respective EPC churches and those who leave internally while remaining, at least on the surface, a part of the Church. But there is also one other group.

The third group is those who care and want to support others in the deserts of faith and church. As Mark said, 'There is a huge gap when it comes to "being there" for people' in the midst of their faith struggles, questions and doubts. The following chapters will help people who want to be alongside others. In *A Churchless Faith* the idea of leaver-sensitive churches – that is, those churches which are open to the concerns and needs of potential church leavers – is explored. I believe there is a huge role for churches and people who will take seriously the faith journeys of the leavers, providing resources, support and companionship as people traverse the difficult places of faith. Philip Richter and Leslie Francis in *Gone But Not Forgotten* retell one of Jesus' parables,[5] saying 'Which of you, having a hundred sheep, if you have lost one of them, does not say: "We can't be bothered to look for strays. We've got a farm to run here! We can't risk the ninety-nine for the sake of just one. If the sheep has gone, it's gone. It's not our fault sheep are silly! We've got other important things to worry about."'[6] The chapters that follow try to give understanding and resources that interested churches could adapt for their own contexts. These resources are for those who recognize that the ones and twos who leave are worth following and that their faith is of primary importance to God and their journeys significant for the future shape of the churches.

Of course this is not the dominant view taken by EPC church leaders. Stereotypes and misunderstandings continue to prevail when it comes to people who leave, or consider leaving, church. Sadly, much blame is put on those who leave and often the only option considered open to them is 'to repent' and come back to the church. Because of this it is important to clearly re-state that the aim of this book is not about getting people back to church or keeping them there: that is a peripheral and secondary concern. Rather we are concerned with each person's faith and how each of us can be 'called again' with authenticity and integrity to the God we, like Mark, once followed with enthusiasm and commitment. Our focus, therefore, will not be 'church' but Christian faith and how that faith is nurtured and developed in the really difficult places. Looking at the book from a church perspective it is for those who leave and those who stay and those who care and want to support others in and through the deserts of Christian faith. This is not an attack on the Church. On the contrary, when you care for something you work for its very best even when that means pointing out weaknesses and striving for change.

The life and work of the French philosopher Paul Ricoeur may help us to cast some light on the way forward. Paul Ricoeur was born in 1913. His mother died a few months after his birth and he and his sister were then brought up by his father until he was called up to fight in the First World War. After a few months his father was listed as missing in action and presumed dead. By then Paul and his sister Alice had been listed as *'pupils de la nation'* (dependent on the state). They went to live with their grandparents until in 1928 his grandmother died, and a few years later in 1933 when Paul was 20 his grandfather also died. In adulthood Paul began a promising career as a philosopher. In 1935 he married Simone and his career was progressing exceptionally well when war intruded again. In 1939 Paul was called up to fight in the Second World War. After a few months in action he was captured and spent nearly five years in a prisoner-of-war camp. Only at the end of the war was he released. On returning home he met his five-year-old daughter for the first time. Having been confronted by so much suffering and evil it is not surprising that these would become dominant themes in his philosophical work and his own reflection. Ricoeur went on to become a famous philosopher, teacher and writer who has greatly influenced French and indeed worldwide philosophical thought.

In his 1967 text on evil entitled *The Symbolism of Evil* Ricoeur speaks of a point 'beyond the desert of criticism, where we wish to be called again'.[7] This means we may be called by God beyond a profound, deep and wide-ranging critique of the Christian faith. In so doing Ricoeur postulates a point beyond criticism where people can be called on in their faith and yet never back to the types and style of faith they left. Paul Ricoeur is a modern Jeremiah as he points to the way many people's faith is both 'uprooted, torn down', 'destroyed and overthrown'. He also points to the possibility that this need not be the end of Christian faith: merely the clearing of the ground of the soul in preparation for God's new 'building and planting'.[8] For Ricoeur the deconstruction of an old faith creates the space from which we can be 'called again', realizing that being 'called again' can never simply mean being called back to the faith we have left.

Ricoeur is exactly the kind of person we need to listen to as we consider the possibility of Christian faith beyond the desert and dark places of faith. Such deserts come in many different forms. For some, they are deserts of critique, as Ricoeur's quote describes, in which our faith is severely critiqued, even deconstructed, theologically, philosophically or through personal despair, doubt, suffering, grief, unanswered prayers and failure.

Ricoeur is an internationally recognized and acclaimed philosopher and so brings a depth of intellectual integrity to the task. He has personally traversed enormous valleys of suffering, struggle, despair and difficulty and it is out of the depths of these that his personal credibility is born. But he is also a man of faith in God who, despite or perhaps because of his enormous intellect and personal experience of despair, has found a plausible faith which is consistent with the scriptures, his strength of philosophical thought and personal experience.

Recently[9] the Pope awarded Paul Ricoeur the Paul VI International Award. In so doing the Pope thanked the French philosopher for the way in which he has worked to harmonize faith and reason. The Pope stressed the way in which Ricoeur's research

> manifests how fruitful is the relation between philosophy and theology, between faith and culture . . . Theology's source and starting point must always be the word of God, yet since God's word is truth, the human search for truth – philosophy, pursued in keeping with its own rules – can only help to understand God's word better.

As Ricoeur received the award his mix of personal experience, philosophical knowledge and compassionate faith were revealed. Speaking about the award, the 90-year-old Ricoeur said, 'The first part of my philosophical work was a reflection on evil . . . In my work, there is a progressive evolution: from a feeling of culpability I have increasingly opened through a particularly painful experience, to that which I would call the culture of compassion. It is an active compassion, which tends to diminish evil.' The outworking of this compassion is shown in Ricoeur's decision to give the award's 100,000 euros to the Fondation John Bost, a French charity that aids the physically and mentally disabled, and people with problems of social integration.

Of course each of our journeys is different. While there is a great deal we can learn from Ricoeur and his life and struggles, they simply act as a guide for our own journeys. They are a framework that may give shape to our own struggles, realizing that each of our questions, doubts, fears, failures, deserts and dark nights of faith are different. God does not work in all our lives in the same way. Each of us is different, and God works in and through our lives in unique ways. Although each year's final examination paper in a course of study can be different, there still remains value in looking at old examination papers to see how it was for those who went before us. In this sense Ricoeur provides us with one previous paper.

This book is for those in the dark and desert places of faith. It attempts to articulate their concerns and provide support for their journeys. The chapters that follow will deal with many of the common concerns and struggles of those traversing the deserts of Christian faith. To find our way we will draw on the stories of contemporary journeyers, characters from scripture and historical guides from the deserts of faith to help light our own paths. While the following chapters are undergirded by substantive research and experience gained from listening to many faith strugglers and church leavers, such research will remain in the background. Our concern is to point to the possibility of robust and genuine Christian faith in and beyond the deserts of faith. The chapters that follow will hopefully present ways towards a robust faith in an increasingly postmodern, post-Christendom context.

In Chapters 2 and 3 we will consider two metaphors used by Christian leaders and mystics for prolonged faith crises. These are the 'desert' and the 'dark night'. Because they are metaphors, more than one can be used. Neither provides a one-to-one match with our personal stories, but they do, in the words of Walter Brueggemann, provide 'an odd, playful and ill-fitting match' to our own reality, 'the purpose of which is to illuminate and evoke dimensions of reality which will otherwise go unnoticed and therefore un-experienced'.[10] Using the catch-cry sparked by Ricoeur that 'in and beyond the deserts of faith we can be called again' we will consider first what it means to thrive in and beyond the desert (Chapter 2) and then what it means to see in and beyond the dark night (Chapter 3). Chapters 4 to 12 pick up successively the themes of questions, truth, prayer, worship, failure, suspicion, belonging, evangelism and mission. These are all important, even key themes of the evangelical church. Yet they are also typically themes that need to be completely reworked, even transformed as people journey through crises of faith. These chapters will hopefully provide a wider canvas of understanding for each of these crucial Christian themes.

2

Thriving In and Beyond the Desert

––––⟨∘⟩––––

In a desert land he found him,
  in a barren and howling waste.
He shielded him and cared for him;
  He guarded him as the apple of his eye.[1]

On our planet of extremes, perhaps the most frightening and fascinating places are deserts. Covering one-fifth of the earth's land surface, they form the harshest and most barren of environments. Inhospitable and seemingly incapable of sustaining anything but the most rudimentary plant and animal life, the deserts are home to 13 per cent of the world's people. The Sahara Desert, for example, covers most of Northern Africa, enveloping more than one-third of the continent, an area greater than the United States of America, accounting for eight per cent of the world's land area. This, the largest of the world's deserts, is a place where temperatures in excess of 55°C have been recorded and where frosts are found in the winter. Rainfall in most parts of the Sahara is scant and erratic, some areas enduring several years without even a hint of a shower. In common with other desert regions, strong, unpredictable winds form typical weather patterns. These winds can blow for days on end, bringing with them vast amounts of dust and sand, which cover everything in their path and reduce visibility down to almost zero. Yet, surprisingly, the Sahara has 1,200 varieties of plants, many only found in the desert.

While physical deserts make up a large part of our physical world, their spiritual equivalents, which we might call 'spiritual deserts', often make up a large part of many people's Christian journeys. A cursory glance at the scriptures reminds us of the regularity and significance of both physical and spiritual deserts in the lives of biblical characters. Throughout the scriptures references to geographical deserts occur over 300 times. Added to these are the passages that speak of exile which Isaiah[2] described as being like a 'motherless child'. These desert, wilderness, exiled times and places connect with the experience of many modern faith strugglers – those people who sense themselves in a wilderness of faith and, like the orphan described by Isaiah, feel abandoned and vulnerable. This deep sense of rootlessness connects closely with many 'postmodern' people's experience of faith.

Early on in the biblical story we meet Abram and Sarai, the parental figures of faith for all Christians, Muslims and Jews alike. Called by God, Abram and Sarai leave their people and their own country to journey into the unknown desert beyond the city of Haran where they had been comfortably settled. The decision to leave the safety and security of the city for the unknown expanse of desert and foreign territory is recorded as God's. Like Abram and Sarai, Moses is also forced into the wilderness and later returns to Egypt at God's direction to lead his own people into the vast unknown and hostile environment of the desert. For many modern Christians, leaving church to enter the unknown and unchartered territory beyond the structures, theology and community of 'church' appears equally as their call by God. Like Jesus, they are called into the desert and, like the desert wanderings of Abram, Moses or the people of Israel, this can often be a long journey in a wasteland. Yet it can also be a journey of tremendous value, personal growth, spiritual depth and encounter with God. For as the physical deserts which appear so bleak and void contain such a richness of life and such vastly different species of plant and wildlife, so too the spiritual deserts contain hidden and often wonderful secrets. In journeying into the heart of the spiritual deserts many modern pilgrims are finding, as Elijah did, that God is already waiting in the desert for them to encounter him in new and richly rewarding ways.

In many evangelical, charismatic and Pentecostal church settings today there is little said about the desert places of faith. The writings of the spiritual leaders of old who traversed intense desert periods are rarely part of EPC church menus. Yet the earliest Christians were well aware of the importance of the deserts – both the physical and spiritual kinds. The early Christian monks were the 'desert fathers' who chose to inhabit the desert land of the Middle

East for many centuries. These desert fathers encouraged people to enter the deserts specifically for the purpose of finding God because they recognized the links between living in a hostile physical desert and the deep spiritual deserts of faith. For them the very dry, arid and seemingly Godless phases of the Christian journey were often seen as parallels to the desert lives they lived. They also knew that as the deserts of the physical earth are vastly different, so too are the spiritual deserts that are part of the Bible, the early Church and the experience of so many of the faithful people of God. Although always personally unique, the desert experiences of faith have formed well-worn paths for the people of God.

The deserts of faith, in their emptiness, barrenness and their sense that God is silent, absent and seemingly disinterested have much in common with many of the experiences of entering a physical desert. Both are scary, lonely, confusing and disorienting places. Entering them is like crossing a threshold of uncertainty, threat and danger. Naturally everything within us recoils from such places.

These wildernesses of faith experienced by so many people today can take on a similar shape and sets of feelings to the physical wilderness that Moses entered. For in both there is a sense of being thrown into a vast and hostile unknown world. With this comes the realization that all that has helped us in the past is now useless, redundant and often completely obsolete. Yet coupled with this is the sense that the only way forward, the only way God wants us to go, is deeper into this harsh and death-like environment of desert. We too can feel like Moses felt, that to go back is to court death – not in our case a physical death, but the death of our faith and the death of our very selves. We may not have opted for this desert existence, but we are here, and being here we are faced with a choice. Will we embrace this new existence or attempt to minimize it, deny it or hasten its end?

This is the point that Russell came to as huge questions and doubts began to surface in his faith and a deep restlessness and dissatisfaction enveloped him. For Russell, this was threatening. He was a full-time, highly committed leader in a Christian organization. There was nowhere to voice safely what he was feeling, nowhere to take his questions and, as he said, 'I remember feeling often that going to church was more than I could handle.'

Russell The real tension was I had this huge emotional commitment to this lifestyle, to my belief system, and I didn't know how to reconstruct my belief system, and it wasn't just an intellectual thing, my life depended on it. I just didn't know what else I was going to do. What would I do with my family? I had two children at that point. What was I going to do?

Snippets from Walt Disney's cartoon film *The Prince of Egypt* provide a good illustration of what it feels like for people like Russell as they enter personal spiritual wastelands. In one of the early scenes in the film we see Moses running into the desert as he flees his old life at Pharaoh's Court. Leaving the life he knew and was comfortable within, he now enters the totally foreign world of the Middle Eastern desert. Sandstorms and thirst, coupled with endless miles of desert, are all that lie before him. He's frightened, and yet knowing that to go back would be certain death, he is forced to move on deeper and deeper into the hostile terrain of the desert. Out in the desert the clothes he wears and the armlets that symbolize his status at Pharaoh's Court are useless. There is a scene in the film where Moses tears them off, throwing them away in disgust. While he was proud of wearing them in Egypt he realizes they are now useless extra weight. Leaving the Air Force a number of years ago I was left with a very similar practical question – what do I do with my uniforms, my rank insignia and my military hats? These were important and highly significant while in the military, but now they are completely redundant, even silly. Many people called into the desert experiences of the Christian faith feel the same sort of experience. The things that were most helpful in building their faith and in drawing them towards God have also now become tired and empty. Moses now needs totally new clothing, new ways of surviving and finding sustenance and new companions. In short, all that helped him and supported him while at Pharaoh's Court has become obsolete, redundant, even a liability. The old life with its skills and ways must be left and a totally new way of living found.

How long was Moses in the desert alone and simply wandering? How close to death from hunger and thirst did he come? What was going on in his mind as he lay on the desert sand? How worn out, depressed, confused, tired and despairing did he become? We don't know, but we can read between the lines that this was a very long journey of struggle and fear; a journey of intense and frightening feelings. As Job reminds us, this is never easy:

> I still rebel and complain against God;
> I can't hold back my groaning.
> How I wish I knew where to find him,
> And knew how to go where he is.[3]

Over the last decade I have talked with many people, both in formal research interviews and informally as a friend or pastor. In these discussions I have heard numerous people describing what the spiritual desert has been like for them. Some of the common experiences spoken of include:

- Losing a sense of identity with God.
- Losing the old landmarks of faith.
- The Bible and prayer appear to go cold and empty.
- Becoming irritated with spiritual talk.
- Becoming acutely aware of failure, weakness, disappointment, of hurting others, and of being personally hurt.
- A conscious sense of going through the motions at church.
- Feeling they don't fit or don't want to fit into church or Christian groups any more.
- A deep grieving for the kind of faith they used to have.
- A sense of panic.
- A desire to blame someone or something.

While not everyone mentions any or all of the feelings above, an almost universal response is, why? Why me? and Why now? This must surely have been the question on Moses' lips as he sat by the well in the desert. It is the question David asks as he flees Saul saying, 'What have I done? What is my crime?'[4] It is also the cry of Job as he asks God, 'Why have you made me your target? Have I become a burden to you?'[5] We could answer that Moses was in the desert because he took the law into his own hands and tried to do what only God could, and perhaps answer David's question by saying it was Saul's doing, not God's; or even explain Job's questioning with the response that God was testing him. Even if we can rationalize why each of these biblical characters wound up in the desert we are still left with Elijah whom the scripture says had

remained faithful to God, and Jesus who was full of the Holy
Spirit, and yet both are led into their respective deserts. Taken
together, the only answer is that many deserts, perhaps most, are
not the result of something we have done or not done. They are not
a punishment for sin or wrong choices in life. For most, the
'Why?' question is left unanswerable. Our cry is mirrored in the
unanswered cry of David, 'Why, Yahweh, do you turn a deaf ear?
. . . Why do you make yourself scarce? . . . The only friend I have
left is the darkness.'[6]

Such feelings, and the dominating question 'Why?' are similar to
the experiences of the famous writer and Christian mystic John
Donne. From a life filled with much suffering he chose to become
an Anglican priest and was appointed priest to St Paul's Cathedral
in 1621 at the time of the Great Plague. Donne, a lifelong melan-
cholic, tormented by the sins of his youth, having failed in all his
ambitions and generally disregarded, didn't seem to be a person
who would be of much help during this dark time. Yet Donne
refused to leave the city as the plague spread and was later to be
diagnosed himself as having the dreaded disease. As he lay sick and
despairing he wrote his *Devotions*, outlining his suffering, his
questions, his taunts of God, his pleading for forgiveness from
God, his dashed hopes. He, like Job, longed for death rather than
carrying on with the suffering he was experiencing. He wrote of
sleep being his only release and then found this too was taken from
him. He pictured himself as a sailor tossed about by the towering
swells of an ocean in storm – a sailor who saw only an occasional
glimpse of a far-away land, only to lose it again as the next giant
wave crashed over him.

Donne began with the 'Why?' question and wondered if it could
be God. Was his illness something God sent? He rightly recoils
from such a deduction and in the end never answers it. 'Although
his *Devotions* do not answer these big philosophical questions it
does record Donne's emotional resolution and a gradual movement
towards peace.'[7] Donne's experience is so similar to many called or
forced into the deserts of faith where the question 'Why?' is yelled
from the depths of the heart and yet so often never answered. At
least it is not answered in an intellectual sense. At times like this we
often seek a deeper meaning: a meaning that can only be conveyed
in image, poetry or story. A modern parable states:

A sheep found a hole in the fence and crept through it. He was so glad to get away and he wandered far and got lost. And then he realized he was lost and being followed by a wolf. For a long time he wandered in the desert, scared, alone, frightened. But the shepherd came and rescued him and carried him to a village and in spite of everyone's urgings to the contrary, the shepherd refused to nail up the hole in the fence.

The story doesn't answer why the shepherd didn't cover up the hole, but it does imply that the journey through the hole was important for the shepherd and for the sheep – so important that it was worth leaving the fence unrepaired and letting others travel a similar path.

If the 'Why?' question is the most common, then the next most common is almost always, 'How long will this go on? When will it end?' Turning to the scriptures again we find this question on David's lips, 'How long, O Lord? Will you hide yourself for ever?'[8] It is also the question on the lips of the people of Israel as they wander endlessly through the desert. And unlike the 'Why?' question, this time there are specific and clear answers given. Moses, we are told, was in the desert for 40 years, as were the people of Egypt. Jesus' time in the desert, on the other hand, was limited to 40 days. What of our own time in the spiritual deserts? While we don't know how long it will last, it is probably safe to anticipate somewhere between the 40 days of Jesus and the 40 years of Moses. Cold comfort, I hear you say. But looking to the end of our own experience of the desert does not seem to be the point. Rather, we need to appreciate, as the biblical characters came to appreciate, that the crucial question is not how to get out of the desert but how to survive and even thrive in the desert. Getting out isn't the aim, neither is counting down the days, as if the experience in the desert is simply a struggle or hardship to be lived through as quickly as possible. Rather we need to find substance for our faith so we can survive, even thrive, in this new hostile and difficult place. This begins by mourning what has been lost and learning to live neither in past memories nor illusionary hopes of the future but in the present moment. It means being still with the pain of these losses. We cannot minimize, suppress or ignore them. We cannot run away from them. All we can do is sit with the pain.

Over time we realize that it is God who has led us. There were undoubtedly various circumstances that got us here; some were within our control and choices, yet there were also many more. Sadly, others may also have been instrumental in forcing us into this new wasteland. Yet the eyes of faith remind us that beyond these personal choices and the actions of others lies the greater purpose of God. The circumstances we can identify as leading to the desert time are the instruments of God. Differentiating what was our choice, the influence and impact of others and what is the quiet orchestration of God is a fruitless task. The real questions we must face are: 'How am I to live here? How am I to grow here? What am I to learn here?'

This means realizing that most desert understanding and truth is counter-intuitive and that our personal growth and learning lies in the least attractive directions. We need the courage to do what we least feel like doing: following a counter-intuitive path. Illustrations of such paths are all around us: the shipwrecked person who does not try and swim for the shore but stays with the upturned boat; the lost hiker who does not frantically try and walk or run but finds shelter, marks her position and settles down to wait for help; the sailor who goes with the storm rather than trying to fight against it; the man swept away by a river and who lets the current carry him to a bank rather than striving for the nearest land; the boy attacked by an angry dog who stands still when every impulse makes him want to run; the first-time abseiler who leans back away from the rock face when her every desire is to hug the rocks; the puppy with a large splinter of glass in its foot who lets someone hurt it further as they dig out the splinter. Acting in a counter-intuitive way always demands determination and courage. We are acting in contradiction to our internal feelings and any sign of progress or positive movement from without. We may not have chosen this desert place; being here we may also not want to opt for a different place, but are we willing to fully choose this desert path? Can we, as the popular church adage says, 'Let go and let God'?

Letting go and letting God can only begin when we cease trying to get out of the desert ourselves: when we accept and even embrace the aridness and difficulty of our present context and cease trying to chase either the experiences of the past or an easy way out. Only then are we ready for the personal and spiritual growth that God desires. Elijah had to accept that God wasn't in the wind or the earthquake or the fire, though these were the places where he, and often we, would like to find God. Most often God does not come to us at these times in dramatic ways. While part of us would like a God who is loud and audible, we see that Elijah came to realize that God was in the still, small and quiet whisper. Chasing the wind and the fire, no matter how impressive, will most probably not lead us to where we can find God.

God will be found in the wilderness in a burning bush, in the quiet, still voice, or on a lonely mountain-top. God is found in the vision of the sea animals of the deep, the stars and the sand of the beaches, as Job found God. God will be found in the desert, in the darkness, in the wilderness, in our grief, despair, disillusionment, in our suffering. Not at our control or because of our efforts, but solely by God, and probably in quite unexpected ways and at unanticipated moments. Not in the big, flash and the beautiful does God tend to meet us, but deeply, simply but profoundly, simply yet personally. Like the psalmist, we may come to say:

> For God alone my soul waits in silence;
>   from him comes my salvation.
> He only is my rock and my salvation,
>   my fortress; I shall not be greatly moved.[9]

Here the psalmist says 'my soul waits in silence'; this silence is common in the desert time. As Doug Reichel wrote of his own personal faith desert, 'I didn't talk much while in the desert because words have a way of shallowing the depth of the agony. Deserts are places to conserve energy, not waste it. So people who are in the desert don't pontificate or analyse, they just plod.'[10]

One of the striking features of Jesus' journey into the desert was the way he co-operated with God in the desert experience. He didn't try to escape it or run from it. Rather, he saw it as part of what God was leading him into and went with it – he let go of his own natural revulsion and desire to escape and let God.

The question, 'What do church leavers need in their own deserts of faith?' formed the basis of a session at a recent conference for spiritual directors. With the help of the spiritual directors, the vast majority of whom knew people with very palpable struggles of faith, we suggested the following list of things that are worth having in the desert experience of faith:

22

- A break from frenetic Christian activity.
- A safe place to explore.
- A clear validation of our own journey.
- A reverence for our journey, for whenever people share the intimate details of their journey of faith we find ourselves on holy ground.
- Help to explore fresh places, images and stories.
- Permission to explore beyond the 'safe' and the known.
- Encouragement to trust our own wisdom.
- Opportunities to tell our developing story and have our story heard.
- A non-judgemental environment.
- To hear our journey normalized but not organized.
- Anchors and handholds for the most difficult terrain. These are normally cut into the rock by previous travellers. Finding such handholds through reading or hearing of the desert journeys of others can be very important.
- Support to ensure we do not underestimate our grief for the loss of past ways.
- Remembering that the deserts and dark nights have been well-worn paths for centuries of Christians.
- Support to create new boundaries.
- Assurance that this is a time of God, not the devil or personal failure.
- Companionship and friendship in the hard places.

This last point is particularly important. In the difficult terrain of our Christian journey we need fellow-travellers. Instinctively however, we often realize that the people we have travelled with in our more fervent days will be of little help. Very often companions don't come from the directions we might have expected. Doug Reichel points this out from his own journey when a Christian leader offers him advice which he characterizes as 'acidic counsel'. He says: 'The proverbial straw that so damaged the camel happened with some specific "words of counsel" from a visiting Christian leader whose insensitive, completely misguided and hurtful words about me and to me left me walking out of our church, knowing that I would not return for a long time.'[11] The same, it seems, happens with the woman in the Song of Songs who in the middle of the night goes looking for her lover, asking help of the watchmen, men she could have expected to help her, and is beaten up by them instead of receiving help. Desert dwellers often find little solace and comfort in their established Christian relationships. As Doug said:

> After walking out of our church I knew that my withdrawal would also be from a close friend for a season. We had met weekly for four years over breakfast to talk, banter ideas, sharpen and pray for each other. But I could not talk or banter or sharpen or pray any more so I wrote him a long letter explaining. He wrote back a card that accompanied a particular wine we had enjoyed together. That card and bottle became for me a moving symbol of all that friendship could be in the darkest hours. It was fleeting, like the scent of roses unexpectedly pushed past your nostrils by a wind gust – but I smelled hope. In the card were written the following words:
>
> 'I respect your need to be silent, to withdraw for a while – I'll be silent with you. Thanks for letting me know why. Please know that I trust you and our friendship. It's hard to be distant, to walk afar off, but we'll weather this new dimension to our friendship. I'm crying silently with you. Please accept this bottle of Pinot Auxerrois as a token of my trust in you and our friendship – and the hug that comes with it.'[12]

Ironically, the companions we find for the journey are often quite different from ourselves. When we look at the desert experiences of the biblical characters we see that God sometimes sent the most unusual people to accompany lonely desert explorers. Melchizedek, surely one of the most mysterious of biblical characters, came to Abram in his desert wanderings. Jethro the Midian priest came to the assistance of Moses. Both of these companions knew the desert and were messengers from God, yet they stood outside of the group Abram or Moses might have expected help to come from. It seems that God continues to work in this way. Many current followers traversing the deserts of faith find God's leading on the lips and in the lives of the most unusual of people. The middle section of the film *The Lion King* illustrates in a humorous and lighthearted way the unusual companions that may be given to us in desert times. The film shows Simba the young lion cub being forced into the desert wastelands where he is befriended by two of the most unusual characters – Pumbaa and Timon. Pumbaa the wart-hog and Timon a meerkat make the most unlikely pair of companions for a lion, but in the desert they are just what he needs.

The film shows the exhausted Simba lying on the parched desert plains with buzzards circling around him when Pumbaa and Timon arrive to his rescue. They, like Jethro's daughters, lead him back to their oasis in the desert and teach him that he 'has to put his past behind him'. Here he learns to laugh and enjoy himself, even to laugh *at* himself. There is a delightful scene as they introduce him to a new diet. When Simba asks his new companions for food he wants zebra or antelope meat but they introduce him to slugs and bugs – a very different and at first unattractive diet but one that later Simba admits is 'slimy but satisfying'. Let's not make too much of a Walt Disney film – it is only an illustration. Yet it is an illustration that in a very simple way points to the power of companions in the wilderness of faith; companions who may be the most unlikely of friends. Companions who, on first impression, we would have discounted. Companions who teach us to live and even enjoy the desert experience and companions who introduce us to a new, perhaps unusual, even 'slimy' but satisfying diet. It is with Pumbaa and Timon in the desert that Simba grows from being a lion cub to adulthood and maturity. This is equally the case for many on the Christian journey. For it is in the wastelands and deserts of our faith that despite their difficulty and harshness we often grow the most. To move from the imagery of Walt Disney to the scriptures – it is so often here that we move from 'milk' to 'meat'.

Melchizedek is the archetypal Pumbaa- and Timon-type figure. He is also the companion sent by God to Abraham at a key point in his own journey. Melchizedek has no genealogy, no father or mother. Instead he simply appears in the narrative as if out of nowhere and disappears in the same way after he has met with Abraham. We know very little about this character whom the biblical record says first introduced God's people to the symbolic meal of bread and wine and to whom Abraham gives a tithe. Although we know little about him, we are told that he was a priest. The word 'priest' means bridge-builder. A priest is therefore someone who bridges the divide between humanity and God. This is what Melchizedek does for Abraham, and he is recorded in the book of Hebrews as a prototype of Jesus the High Priest.

While the companions sent by God may be significant friends and guides along our desert path, the key person we long to meet isn't Pumbaa, Timon, Melchizedek or an angel, but God. This was the experience of Moses and Abram and Sarai. For God met them in their personal deserts. But God did not meet them immediately or at a timing of their choice. In fact for much of the desert time they were deafened not by God's words but by God's silence. Moses too seemingly waits in silence for some time, in his case some years. When God came to him it was in a totally unexpected and new way. Moses remembers this later, saying,

> In a desert land he found him,
> in a barren and howling waste.
> He shielded him and cared for him;
> He guarded him as the apple of his eye.[13]

Whether we are led into the deserts of criticism, despair, doubt, disillusionment, suffering, sickness, pain, grief, failure, or some personal combination of these and others, God longs to meet us there. If God does meet us the means through which God does this are as unique as the deserts themselves; no two journeys are ever the same. While we cannot predict the means God may use to encounter us, we can anticipate that it will probably not be in the ways we would expect or plan. The prophet Isaiah promises the same for those who journey into the darkness (another metaphor for the hard times of faith) recording God's words:

> I will give you the treasures of darkness,
> riches stored in secret places,
> So that you may know that I am the LORD,
> the God of Israel, who calls you by name.[14]

Even this encounter with God is not a universal experience, neither is it the fundamental point of the desert experience. Doug Reichel sums up what he gained from his desert experience, saying:

1 *Deserts help us grow up.* Deserts are 'adult' places that reveal childish, immature notions about God. Notions like if I do this, God will do this . . .

2 *Deserts expose deception.* They reveal our cherished illusions about life, ourselves and others for what they are – illusions. The desert 'dis-illusions'.
3 *Deserts birth realness.* Shedding illusions leaves us with a yearning for authenticity in all areas of life . . .
4 *Deserts clarify priorities.*
5 *Deserts purify desires.* We are drawn into different personal deserts of the heart for the purpose of being liberated from our seductive and addictive desires.[15]

A quick look at this list reminds us that what is gained in the desert times is not answers to our questions or wonderful encounters with God; rather the key focus of our time in the deserts and wildernesses of faith is the bringing of change: change in ourselves; change that is best described as transformation. In the deserts of faith progress is measured not so much by what we know or by what we experience but by how God is transforming us. If we look back to John Donne we see his journal writings moving him from asking 'Why this pain?' to 'How could this pain redeem?' That is, how could this pain change him and those around him? It means coming to value the fact that the desert is measured not by length, darkness, knowledge or the experience of meeting personally with God, but by the degree to which we are changed.

Saying the desert is a place of personal change or transformation is hard to swallow when our own loss and discomfort is so large and in our face. For some, the changes are simply too slow. This may motivate them to either jump back into the old ways of doing church and being a Christian or push them away from Christians and Christian things altogether. If these are the two obvious extreme possibilities (go back to your old ways of faith or ditch faith) it must seem a very difficult and hopeless choice. Put simply, lose your faith or your sense of integrity and self-development. Is there no third way?

'*Instrumentum conjunctum cum Deo*' – an instrument shaped to the contours of the hand of God. This is the ultimate purpose of the desert journey. The third way. The way which shifts our focus from what we may learn or gain to what God is doing with us for God's own purposes.

'*Instrumentum conjunctum cum Deo*' describes a wonderful point in the Christian life. The point where we become willing and useful instruments in the purposes of God. We become instruments that God has fashioned and prepared for personal use. St Ignatius knew that God wants to shape us ready for the Spirit to use as favoured instruments; instruments that fit perfectly the hand and purpose of God. Father Thomas Green[16] illustrates '*Instrumentum conjunctum cum Deo*' by considering the favoured knife of the butcher, the knitting needles of the knitter or the pen of the writer. In each case a particular 'tool' which has been used again and again becomes the favoured choice of the worker because they fit so neatly in the worker's hand. Over time they have been moulded and shaped to better fit the crafter's hand. And whether we think of the knife of the butcher, the knitting needle of the knitter or the pen of the writer, we realize these tools of choice are often not the most attractive or expensive of the instruments available to the worker but they are his or her first choice and the most trusted. The deserts, if we go with them, ultimately shape us to be the '*Instrumentum conjunctum cum Deo*' of the Lord Almighty. Instruments that God can use. Instruments that through constant wear and usage have become a perfect fit for the hand of God. This is not always, or probably ever, an easy process, as rough edges are worn smooth as constant use wears them down. Yet surely it is better to be the instrument of choice and a better fit in the Master's hand than remain in a pristine and unused state in a plastic wrapper. For we are formed and shaped through life to be willing instruments in the hand of God, and in the end while we are being shaped to better fit God's purposes we have birthed within our very selves and souls new depths of hope, faith and love.

3

Seeing In and Beyond the Dark

————◄○►————

Job said:
I long for the past,
    when God took care of me,
and the light from his lamp
    showed me the way through the dark.[1]

Archbishop Desmond Tutu is known for his sense of humour, his broad smile, radiant hope and unwavering faith. Yet he is a man who knows the depths of despair. He knows the despair of the long years of oppression under the regime of apartheid. He knows the despair of friends and colleagues beaten, imprisoned and killed by an unjust governmental system. He knows the despair of the stories told at the 'Truth and Reconciliation Commission'. He knows a parent's despair of seeing his own 'dearly loved' son choosing a life he does not understand and grieves over. And he knows the personal despair of being diagnosed with a potentially terminal illness. At this personal level, in his own family, in his health and through the long years of fighting oppression and the horrors of racial hatred, Archbishop Tutu knows despair. And yet despite all that he has experienced and all that he has heard and seen he remains a man of hope, lightness and laughter. He is a man, described in a recent interview, as engaging, life-giving and full of hope. How can these two realities coalesce in the one man at the same time?

This is the dilemma reiterated in the words of Paul:

> And so we boast of the hope we have of sharing God's glory!
> We also boast of our troubles, because we know that trouble
> produces endurance, endurance brings God's approval, and his

approval creates hope. This hope does not disappoint us, for God has poured out his love into our hearts by means of the Holy Spirit, who is God's gift to us.[2]

How can Paul boast of troubles and hope at the same time? How can despair and such hopefulness exist in Desmond Tutu at the same time? Are Paul and Archbishop Tutu simply paying lip service to hope or are we to resolve the seeming tension by saying these are extraordinary people who are able to live in a way that we cannot; either because of their personal strength and optimism or because of some special charism of the Spirit? Neither option is satisfying. In this chapter we will consider this seemingly insoluble dilemma by using two images. The first is the image of a knot and is drawn from Paul Ricoeur's writings. The second is an image used by St John of the Cross to illustrate what we called in the last chapter the 'deserts of faith' and this is the image of a dark night.

Paul Ricoeur, as we saw in Chapter 1, is someone like Desmond Tutu and St Paul: someone who knew what personal suffering and the full impact of evil can do to a person. Ricoeur's own life was full of suffering and disaster. He has been shaped through the grief of childhood, the suffering of spending years in a POW camp, the loneliness of separation from family, the hard years of academic study, critical reflection on his ideas and personal loss. Yet as a person of faith and as a philosopher he asks us to consider the possibility that we may be called again beyond the desert of criticism. In other words, the desert is not something to be avoided or hurried through but the context in which we may be called again by God to a new, deeper way of faith. Ricoeur illustrates this call through his 'knot of reality'. This knot is illustrated by tying two ends of rope together. One strand of rope represents the reality of a person's suffering, difficulty and despair, the other their sense of hope and faith in God. But when we talk of the sense of hope and faith in God we cannot think of a naïve or 'pre-critical hope'. Ricoeur makes it clear that for many people evil, suffering and despair have destroyed a naïve hope and a naïve or pre-critical faith. Perhaps this is even a function of evil, suffering and despair? Ricoeur is quite clear in saying that once a naïve faith or hope has been destroyed we can never go back to it and be satisfied. This implies we can never go back to a primitive naïveté of faith and be satisfied. Not at all. When a previous stage or phase of faith begins to break down and we begin to move beyond it into a desert of faith something is lost; irredeemably lost. Yet in and beyond this place of lost-ness we may be called again.

This is what Russell experienced as his own faith began to unravel around him and he looked to the church and the Christian organization that he worked for to help:

> *Russell* The help was psychologically really inadequate . . . I didn't want anyone to tell me what to do, I wanted to be understood, to have my pain heard. But there was no legitimate way of actually expressing my pain . . . I remember having this wonderful thought. I was depressed; I could name it – this nameless thing, this emptiness, this hollowness, this amorphous shapeless thing that was nevertheless real . . . I remember feeling often that going to church was more than I could handle. I think because, it was a funny thing, because it was so nameless. There was a deep sense of frustration, of being there before and having done it all. Occasionally I'd get up and lead the worship, although I would be reluctant to do so at this stage . . . I think I was just running out of energy. But at the same time it was so un-fresh, we would sing the same songs and hear the same prophecies, thousands and thousands of times and the same sermons, just using a different verse. It was thoroughly inadequate. It certainly didn't deal with where we were at. It wasn't scratching where we were itching.

Russell had lost something. What he had lost, Ricoeur tells us, is 'the immediacy of belief . . .' and while having left a naïveté of faith we can never go back to it and be satisfied, 'we can aim at a second naïveté in and through criticism'.[3]

In other words, our personal encounter with evil, suffering and despair can destroy a naïve and pre-critical faith but there still lies open to us an alternative faith. This faith Ricoeur calls a 'second' or 'post-critical' naïveté: a second naïveté which is created through the forming of a knot of realities; the reality of all the pain, suffering and despair that lies within and around us tied to the reality of a deep faith in God. This is a faith that brings hope precisely and only within the depths of the despair that we are facing. The bringing together and holding together of these two strands is what forms the knot of faith. Ricoeur uses the image of this knot of faith to explain the role of both our hope and faith in

God and the role of questioning and doubt or despair in our lives. With both strands of rope clearly in sight we develop what might be called double vision. This is the 'third way' which sees both the stark realities of life and the promises and reality of God and sees them intimately intertwined and linked.

The typical response of many is to come to the point Russell reached where their own naïve faith has been destroyed by despair, suffering and doubt and then be faced with an either/or choice. We could choose to ignore the depths of despair or suffering and to pretend they don't exist. Sadly, this is often the option chosen by many sincere people of Christian faith. Overwhelmed by the reality of our suffering and the crumbling of our naïve faith in response to such suffering we can choose to jettison our faith. But what Ricoeur's knot of faith points us to is a third option: the option of bringing together two seemingly contradictory realities and working to tie them together into a knot that affirms both realities alongside and interconnected with each other. To do so is to begin the process of forming a second naïveté of faith – a post-critical faith. It is something we can only do in the midst of suffering, despair and doubt.

Ricoeur's knot is a powerful image. I have used it with a group of spiritual directors at their biannual conference and also in front of a congregation in a Sunday morning service. While explaining what the two strands of rope represent, I have tied the ends together by lying the pieces of rope alongside each other and then over the top of each other, forming a reef knot. This knot is simple but strong and it is completely immovable regardless of the pressure put on it. The knot shows the reality of despair and suffering and the reality of a post-critical faith lying alongside each other, entwined with each other and together forming a strong knot. It is a knot that could never be formed by one strand on its own. In both settings the image conveyed a powerful spiritual reality to the people watching. Perhaps this same power is conveyed in the enduring Christian symbol of the Celtic knot 'whose spirals intertwine endlessly to symbolise God's encircling protection of his people, to symbolise eternity and to suggest the movement, pilgrimage and progress that is essential to Christian life'.[4]

Such a knot reflects the journey of Alexander Solzhenitsyn who once wrote, 'Bless you, prison . . . for it was in you that I discovered that the meaning of earthly existence lies, not as we have grown used to thinking, in prospering, but in the development of the soul.' It was in prison that Solzhenitsyn learnt this. It was in speaking of the prison that he said 'Bless you'.

But how can this be? How can we find a genuine hope in the midst of our own despair? The image of the knot reminds us that we cannot ignore either the reality of our despair or the reality of faith in God. To dispel one in favour of the other may be easier and quicker but it is ultimately meaningless and leaves us without the foundations we need for living. For many people overwhelmed by despair and suffering, their faith in a God who cares and is involved in the world ends up being jettisoned. Yet this path leads nowhere. There is little hope without God. The philosopher who wrote the book of Ecclesiastes expressed this eloquently more than 3,000 years ago when he pointed to the hopelessness of wealth; and he knew because he was the wealthiest man for his time and area. He points to the hopelessness of wisdom – and with good reason, for he was known as a very wise man who had available the best wisdom of his time. He points to the pointlessness of sex – and he was a man with hundreds of concubines. He points to the pointlessness of merriment and eating and drinking – and he had every opportunity to party day in and day out. The writer had analysed the world around him and reflected deeply on how short and contradictory human life is, with its mysterious injustices and frustrations, and concludes 'life is useless'. In the end it is all 'useless, useless . . . Life is useless, all useless'.[5]

If we end our faith in God we will find no hope, no way forward and no purpose or motivation for living without God. As Huston Smith, the world-renowned writer and teacher on world religions, states, we humans are theomorphic creatures – 'ones whose *morphe* (form) is *theos* – God encased within it. Having been created in the *imago Dei*, the image of God, all human beings have a God-shaped vacuum built into their hearts.'[6] Yet equally, as Paul wrote, 'if our hope in Christ is good for this life only and no more, then we deserve more pity than anyone else in all the world'.[7] Take God out of the picture, take eternity out of our frame of reference and there is no hope. There can be no hope. Evil and death destroy everything, and in the words of Solomon we may as well 'eat, drink and be merry for tomorrow we die'. We come to the point the disciples came to when Jesus asked the disciples if they too were going to leave him and 'Simon Peter answered, "Lord, there is no one else that we can go to! Your words give eternal life. We have faith in you."'[8]

While simply abandoning the faith quest leads nowhere, the opposite direction in which we seek to hold on to a naïve faith in God, unpunctuated by the hardships, injustices and unanswerable questions of life, is equally empty. A faith that denies the depths of the human reality, suffering, despair and doubt we have personally experienced ends up consigning us to a very unreal fantasy land – one which bears little or no reality to our own lives and the lives of others. This is the kind of fantasy land Karl Marx so rightly exposed. Marx highlighted the impoverishment of the faithful peasant who was encouraged to endure suffering now and hope in eternity, calling such a promise the 'opium of the people'. A promise that removed them from the realities of their very real situations and suffering yet changed nothing. The only hope he saw such people being offered was effectively saying, 'Yes, it's horrible and unjust now but after death there is your reward. So place your hope in eternity.' And while eternity has always been part of the Christian story, it is not the whole story. For to say this alone is to imply that God has abandoned us to this dark and evil planet and to death, and we will only understand or have relief from this suffering in eternity where God is active in a way God is not active in the here and now. But this cannot be the Christian message – a part does not make the whole. On the contrary, we are told 'the Word became a human being and, full of grace and truth, lived among us. We saw his glory, the glory which he received as the Father's only Son.'[9] This opening passage in the Gospel of John reminds us that God has entered our world and reality and is involved in it. God has not chosen to stand on the sidelines and simply cheer on the players. Rather, God has entered the field of play. Both a post-critical faith and the depth of our own reality have to be owned and explored. We have to work with the Spirit to lay these realities together, to intertwine them in our lives. It is to personally tie the knot of post-critical faith described by Ricoeur.

This juxtaposition of opposites is at first very difficult and counter-intuitive but it leads to a much deeper understanding and foundation for faithful living. It is in fact the only option that allows for personal integrity, continued faith and a genuine encounter with the dark realities of life. The knot that we tie combines authentically alongside each other the struggles and suffering we experience in life and faith in God. The knot is one image of the means through which faith and real life are brought together to provide hope in our despair. The second image we need to consider is an alternative metaphor for what we called 'the spiritual desert' in the previous chapter where we introduced the imagery of a desert as a way of explaining the times of deep criticism, doubt and despair that are common to the journey of faithful following of Christ. In this chapter I want to turn to a different image – the image of a dark night. This is the image chosen by the great spiritual leader of the Christian journey, St John of the Cross.

Imagine, if you will, that the darkness, or the dark night, is our despair, our fear, our anxiety, our sense of hopelessness. As we move forward I do not want to underestimate or diminish to even a minute degree the depth of the darkness that surrounds us. We do not have to lessen or minimize the darkness in order for the light to shine. In fact that is quite the opposite of what we will propose. For the light of Christ is seen in the darkness. Not after we leave the darkness. Not if we survive the darkness. And nor does the light replace the darkness; rather the light shines in the darkness.

The Gospel of John introduces us to the God who enters the world by saying that Christ comes as light into the darkness of the world. 'The light shines in the darkness, and the darkness has never put it out.'[10] Claiming that this Light – Christ – enters the darkness again does not underestimate the depth and power of the darkness. What is being claimed is that the Light comes in the despair and darkness. Whatever the specific darkness may be in our own individual lives, this passage suggests that God comes as light in our darkness and the Light will never be put out by the darkness. As the darkness surrounds us, enveloping us in fear and uncertainty, a long, arduous journey begins. Mike Riddell describes what may lie ahead, saying:

> the dark days are just beginning. Before you emerge into the light again you will be stripped to the core. You will rage and scream at God. You will retreat into a cocoon of sorrow and breathe in slow motion. The colour will drain from the sky, the

meaning from life. As a plough tears through hard earth, your heart will be broken up. You will make friends with pain, nursing it as the child of grief. Utter emptiness fills the earth, and the valley appears to contain nothing but the echo of your own cry. Surely God has left you. The road which seemed to be heading somewhere has become a dead end. A mocking maze with no exit.

Then, one morning in the distant future, you wake and hear a bird singing . . .[11]

For some people there is light after the darkness and the birds do sing again in the distant future, but for others the darkness becomes reality. It becomes our present reality, the only reality we have for now, and for all we know this present darkness is our unending reality. Saying there is light when you exit the tunnel is of little help when you are deep within it.

St John of the Cross teaches that when despair and suffering, evil and even ultimately death face us there is no point trying to run away. The darkness is real and we must go into it. We must face it. John knew the darkness and loved the darkness. His life was marked by personal pain and God's love. John's father chose to marry an orphan girl whom his family saw as below his status and roots, and he was therefore disinherited. He died soon after their third son, John, was born. After his father's death the young family was forced on to the streets, moving from place to place in search of work. John was eventually found a place in an institute for disadvantaged children until in his early teens he found work as 'a nurse-cum-porter' in a hospice for people dying from syphilis. At 21 he left the hospice and joined a community of friars, later training for three years to be ordained as a priest. Many years later, innocently caught in political battles within the Order, he was arrested, imprisoned and subjected to emotional and physical abuse.

> Hour upon hour of interminable blindness, blackness, in a stuffy hole intended as a visitors' toilet. The midday ray of light that poked through a slit high up in the wall served mainly to mock the prisoner, as it passed on and pushed him back into twenty-three more hours of heartless obscurity . . .[12]

It is from this experience that John writes of the 'dark night of the soul': not only the physical suffering and darkness but also the inner darkness as he felt God withdraw and leave him in his despair. Matthew describes this period in John's life:

> Here John was a child. He had been hauled beyond the threshold of his own resources, taken to those outer limits where the only alternatives are a Spirit who fills, or chaos. It was as if the anaesthetic which normal life provides had worn off, his inner self had been scraped bare, and he now ached in a way he never had before for a God who was utterly beyond him. This was the real wound, and it drew from him a raw cry, 'Where are you?'

> > Where have you hidden
> > Beloved, and left me groaning?
> > You fled like a stag
> > Having wounded me;
> > I went out in search of you, and you were gone.[13]

He was forced to face this darkness. 'That is John's greatest gift: not so much to tell us what to do nor to pinpoint our place on the map, but to draw back the curtains and disclose the whole journey as real.'[14] We too cannot pretend that our own darkness does not exist, is not real. Quite naturally and unashamedly, none of us enters the darkness easily. We all fight the darkness and this is normal, even encouraged by God. When periods of 'darkness' come on us we all long for the time before the darkness appeared. We all instinctively want to go back to when it was easier, clearer and less painful. Though we can long for the time before the darkness and grieve for our loss, eventually we must either accept that the daylight has gone or we try to deny the darkness by making our own light to drive it away. Metaphorically we can pull out our torch, or light a candle or start a fire in an attempt to drive the darkness away. Yet in the end our torch batteries will run out, our candle blows out and our fire burns away; then we have no choice but to face the darkness head on. Yet in the darkness we come to see. Slowly, gradually we come to see in the dark and as we begin to see in the dark we realize the warning from Isaiah for those who try to bring their own manufactured

light into the darkness: 'But see here, you who live in your own
light, and warm yourselves from your own fires and not from
God's, you will live among sorrows.'[15]

Sometimes at night I need to get out of bed and go to the toilet
or let the cat out. When I have to get up I always close one eye
before turning on a light. It is a trick I learnt in the Air Force while
on my basic officer training. Our Flight Sergeant for night manoeuvres was a highly esteemed ex-Vietnam veteran. He taught us
that our night vision takes 20 minutes or more to reach its full
effect and that perhaps our best night vision is only achieved after
two hours of being in the dark. After this time our eyes have
become fully acclimatized to the darkness and our pupils are fully
open. Having slowly reached this degree of night sight even a short
glimpse of light can take us back to where we were two hours
before. On night manoeuvres the Flight Sergeant never allowed us
to turn on a torch or to look at any other light source. To do so
would be to lose our night vision. When we stopped to read a map
only one person looked at the map with the torch on and even then
only with one eye closed and if possible a hand over the closed
eyelid. That's why when I get up at night I still close one eye. It
means that when I've let the cat out I can turn the light out, and
change the eye I have open, retaining my night vision in one eye.
This makes it easier to find my way back to bed without walking
into something. Besides being useful advice for those who have to
get up in the middle of the night, the story also illustrates how we
find our way in the dark times of the faith journey.

When we move from a well-lit area into the darkness we are
often effectively blinded in the dark. With our eyes adjusted for
light we cannot see in the dark and it takes quite some time for
them to readjust. But if we wait we realize we can see more in the
dark – far more than we at first expected. It is like this when we
venture from a well-lit room to go outside and look at the night
sky. As our eyes adjust we can see more and more of the stars. We
also become more aware of just how dark it is, but the darkness is
punctuated by the light of countless stars. We come to see what St
John of the Cross talks about. The darkness is not totally dark
after all. It is the same in the dark nights of faith. At first we sense
that God is completely absent, that God has deserted us in our
dark night, but slowly we come to realize that God is not absent.
God is there but we couldn't recognize God or see God at work in

the darkness. We cannot sense God because we are used to God coming in a particular way. Now that way is void and empty, but God nevertheless comes to us in new ways – if we can only perceive them. It is not that God is totally absent. Rather we lack the sight to see God, or to change the image we lack the tongue to taste the things of God and the language to hear what God is saying to us. In the darkness we must let our eyes adjust as slowly we begin to see the light. Like the darkest of real nights, the light of the stars is there but so often our eyes need time to adjust in order to be able to see them.

Streaming across the darkness is the light whose source is millions, perhaps even billions, of years old. This light now reaches us to light our night and guide our path. So too the specks of God's light in the dark nights of faith stream across the centuries offering hope, courage and faith, and perhaps, even more importantly, comfort and care in our hurt, confusion and fear. The light in the dark night of faith that God sends is like the stars on a dark clear night – beautiful, intricate and awe-inspiring.

Once we are aware of what St John of the Cross is pointing to, our struggle is less about understanding what could be happening to our faith and more about allowing the darkness to become our reality. To really accept, even embrace our darkness and despair takes both courage and time. It doesn't mean grovelling in our personal darkness but it does mean owning it for what it is in the hope that, as Jesus said, 'the truth will set you free'.

In fact the advice of the Christian mystics like St John of the Cross is that if God makes it dark, our task is to make it darker. In other words, rather than trying to flee the darkness or find our own artificial means of light we are called to journey into darkness. To quote Father Thomas Green, 'rather than seeking to return to the natural light by which we had previously lived, we must embrace the darkness and positively co-operate with the work of the Holy Spirit in us'.[16]

We have a deck at our home which overlooks part of the city, the airport and the southern coastline. At night we can go out on to this deck and look at the scene and the night sky. The night view is captivating; always changing and often so still. On a good night when the sky is clear we can see quite a few stars, each one a glorious dot of light in the darkness beyond. Recently, while away in a very remote part of the country, we were walking home one night. Without the lights of the city, street lights and the airport it was so much darker. Ironically, because it was so much darker the stars were so much brighter and we were able to see so many more stars, including some which appeared very faint. These stars are also shining above our home but we can't see them. Why? We can't see them because it isn't dark enough.

It is the same with the dark nights of the Christian faith. Only in entering the darkness further, only in embracing the darkness rather than running from it can we see the light that shines in the darkness. If it isn't dark enough the light will not be visible. It is there. The light is always there but we can only come to see it in the darkness.

It is the same with New Zealand's national icon the kiwi. The kiwi is a flightless nocturnal bird. Today anyone wanting to see a kiwi has to go into a nocturnal house at a zoo or wildlife sanctuary. When you enter the nocturnal house it takes a while for your eyes to adjust, but once they have and provided it is dark enough the kiwis will come out of their hideaways to hunt for food. Turn the light on and they retreat back to the safety of the shadows. Finding God in the dark times of our Christian journey is like seeing kiwis or stars: you have to do it in the dark.

The image of the dark night conveys another spiritual truth. The light we see in the night sky is actually very old. It is not an immediate light but rather one that has been travelling for hundreds, thousands, even millions of years. So too the light we often see in the dark nights of faith. The light God sends our way is often not God's own immediate presence but the work, word and wonder of God emanating from the past. The light of God that shines in our darkness and lights our path forward is from the past. In the Old Testament the followers of God were told that they could never look on God's face and live. All, even the ones God was most intimate with, saw only God's back. They were only permitted to see where God had been. Is this the way God works today as well? Is the light he sends us in the dark nights of our own faith journey also the light emanating from where God has previously been? I suspect it is. While we would like a direct, immediate and personal encounter with God, we may find we are also only invited to see where God has been. Using the Old Testament imagery we can see only God's back.

When we go up on the deck at home most often the clearest

thing we can see is the moon. It depends on the time in the moon's cycle, but often the moon is the brightest light in the night sky. On a night with a clear sky and a full moon the light from the moon is enough for me to find the way down our paths or hold a conversation with a friend while still seeing the expressions on their face. Yet the moon is a dark body. It emits no light whatsoever. All the light we see coming from the moon is reflected light. It is in fact the sunlight shining on the moon and then being reflected to us in the darkness of the night when the sun itself is hidden from view. Here too lies the kernel of a spiritual reality. For it is often the same in the dark nights of our faith in which God's reality, truth, hope and love are reflected to us by dark stars: sometimes from the least expected source. So often we ignore this light because we do not anticipate that God could use that source to light our way. In our lives the dark stars that reflect the light of God to us can be people, often the ones we least expect like Melchizedek or the lives of others told through biographies, so-called 'secular' music or disciplines of study. For it would seem that part of what the Holy Spirit is showing us in the times of darkness is that God is at work in places and ways we would not previously have considered or thought possible.

There are stars or sacraments out there that we would normally not perceive as the conveyors of God's love, truth and hope to us. The common definition of a sacrament from both the Reformed and Roman Churches is that 'of an outward and visible sign, ordained by Christ, setting forth and pledging an inward and spiritual blessing'. It begs the question, what are the sacraments in our lives? Those outward and visible signs that God is using to convey an inward and spiritual blessing to us.

I believe it was Teilhard de Chardin who said, 'In all those dark moments, O God, grant that I may understand that it is you who are painfully parting the fibres of my being in order to penetrate to the very marrow of my substance.'

Entering the darkness is difficult. Leaving the light of day is desperately hard. For in the darkness we grieve for all that has been lost. We naturally try to find our way out or find an artificial light for ourselves. We have no idea of how long the night will last. For some people the night doesn't come to an end. It perpetuates and enfolds us, driven often by depression, grief, confusion, doubt and despair. Yet in the darkness God is at work. For the light shines in the darkness and the darkness will not overcome it. Slowly the night we have dreaded and fought against becomes our friend. It is only as we move forward into the dark and embrace it that we see the light of God. Remembering that often the light we see is the light of God's past word and work or light from dark stars; yet it is enough light, maybe just enough, to guide our path and offer us hope.

And maybe this is all Jesus had as he traversed the minefield of expectations, people's pain, institutional injustice and evil. As George Armstrong wrote about Jesus he saw:

> through all this turbulence, Jesus remained 'his own person'. Saddened though he was by the weakness of his disciples and friends, he intelligently analysed what they were experiencing. Though inwardly he knew his own fear, despair and god-forsakenness, he stood his ground. Jesus was no superstar. He did not pull himself up by sheer will-power. He got his courage and his sanity from staying close to God, like a child instinctively stays close to mother or father. From this he found enough strength – perhaps just enough – to keep him going creatively.
>
> A soft salvation and a cheap grace are little use to people who have to carry heavy burdens in life. Jesus is not offering people some easy refuge, rather Jesus is discovered in the midst of the worst of life, only such a suffering and courageous God can help.[17]

It is this God who has walked in the darkest nights of many previous journeyers who offers to be with us in our own personal darkness.

4

Questions In and Beyond Answers

———<o>———

Be patient toward all that is unsolved in your heart and try to love the questions themselves. Do not now seek answers, which cannot be given you because you would not be able to live them. And the point is, to live everything, live the questions now. Perhaps you will gradually, without noticing it, live along some distant day into the answer.

(Rainer Maria Rilke)[1]

Brenda is young, intelligent and passionate about life. Raised in a Christian home, she was deeply committed to her faith and heavily involved in her church for many years until at university a number of questions began bubbling within her.

> *Brenda* I have so many questions regarding my faith, scripture and church. They are genuine questions, questions that have had me in tears of frustration for the last couple of years.

These questions drove Brenda to read and attend seminars and discussion groups in her search for 'honest discussion with people who aren't scared to ask the big questions'.

> *Brenda* I long to talk with someone who won't throw out Sunday school lines like Band-Aids. Who won't think I'm a borderline Christian or spiritually 'not in a good place' if I dare to doubt.

Although she had many questions she wasn't actually after answers:

Brenda I'm not looking for a clued-up person who will make everything clear for me, because I am quite sure they do not exist. I would love someone to feel comfortable talking to me and bashing ideas around, even if they're not 'theologically sound'. It would be good to know that other Christians were secure enough to be real with me, to be vulnerable and to join me in my search for spiritual reality.'

Unfortunately this wasn't what she found among Christian people:

Brenda I got a shock. I found that people don't like difficult questions, they aren't safe and they aren't nice, and it is much better to pretend that everything is OK than to ask 'dodgy' questions. My experience has been that if no pat answers are available, the question is usually disregarded. Some people were honest, saying they would rather not think about such questions. That they are comfortable the way they are, that I should just have faith or pray more for answers or, as one significant church leader kindly warned me, 'If you rock the boat too hard it will flip over.'

As Brenda thought about the attitudes of friends and church leaders the words of an old song seemed to ring true:

Brenda Oh the days when I drew lines around my faith, to keep You out, to keep me in, to keep things safe. Oh the sense of my self-entitlement, to say who's wrong and won't belong and cannot stay.

In a world full of questions, what Brenda found was a church that only had answers. Brenda is not alone. Like Brenda, William and Jennifer were brought up in Brethren churches. They too had fathers as elders, and all were very much involved in church life and strongly committed to their faith until some serious questions about prayer and how God works began to be raised for them.

William There were a lot of things that had been there for many years. There were questions that we probably always had but just couldn't express or even acknowledge to ourselves, because it just wasn't done. You didn't question things in the church. Not things that are really basic to the Christian faith. You just don't question them. If there was a doubt there you get rid of it. Like I could never accept that

God was going to send so many people to hell . . . the vast majority are going to go to hell. I just couldn't accept that. There was no way, in my sense of fairness, that a loving God could do that.

Jennifer Well, you couldn't really get past the traditional answers. And I don't think William could dare look outside of those.

William It was OK to question things on the periphery of church, that were not key to faith, but there was no way you would dare get into the nitty gritty and question those sorts of things. So I think we probably had those sorts of questions and doubts for a long time.

Speaking of her Christian family's reaction when Jennifer and William left church, Jennifer said:

Jennifer Probably they found it very hard to accept, and I found that difficult because of wanting to be accepted. So I really struggled with that. I think I progressed on to a point where I felt comfortable. That this was actually OK with God, it was acceptable. I guess seeing things is part of the journey. This was part of my journey, not something to struggle against.

In EPC churches it would seem answers hold a very important place, while questions are generally treated with much greater suspicion. In this sense EPC churches tend to share a different ethos from that espoused by the popular culture, as illustrated by the character of Commander Ben Sisko in *Star Trek: Deep Space Nine*: 'It is the unknown that defines our existence; we're constantly seeking not just answers to our questions, but for new questions. We are explorers.' This is a very different ethos from that which we find in a typical EPC church. For while the wider culture may be encouraging and fuelling people's questions and exploration of issues, faith and spirituality, the ethos in EPC churches tends to discourage open voicing and discussion of faith-and-life questions. This is particularly true, as William said, when it comes to the underlying foundations of the Christian faith. Yet Mary Tuomi Hammond, an American minister who works with people she calls 'dechurched' says: 'If people cannot speak openly in church and ask their questions, express their doubts, tell their stories – they will go elsewhere to find authentic community and support.'[2]

Over the last five years we have provided discussion and exploration groups for church leavers and people struggling within the Christian faith. Repeatedly we have found that it is the so-called 'basics' of the faith that people want to talk about most. The topics that really captivate people's attention are ones like: What is the nature of God? Who was Jesus? Does prayer work? Communicating with God – what do we hope for? Our images of God: are they life-giving or life-inhibiting? These are the questions people seem to want to discuss – not big ethical or philosophical issues. The everyday issues of 'God and my faith' are the focus for such discussions.

> *Anne-Marie* I strongly believe that doubt is not indicative of a faith
> that is weak. Doubt is inevitable. It's human and it's honest. To have
> the freedom to voice that doubt without being judged is so
> important. To have the courage to explore the doubt, that is what
> gives faith its strength. Faith has to be dynamic, not static, because
> life grinds on and its experiences continually mould us. Our faith has
> to be able to incorporate what we experience of our world, otherwise
> it is based on nothing that has any meaning to us.

These 'basic' or fundamental questions of faith and life are not to be feared or shied away from, but through grappling with these very issues a context is created from which faith can grow, identity can be strengthened and belief matured. The questions themselves can act as stepping stones for our journey. Without the opportunity to wrestle with these questions, people at certain points of the Christian faith are effectively denied the very stepping stones that will allow them to move forward.

Sometimes, but less often than we would like, these questions are also the context from which answers are found. We see both in the scriptures. Thomas got his answer; Job didn't. In their confusion, doubt and despair, both pressed their questions on God. Thomas was very direct: 'Unless I see the scars of the nails in his hands and put my finger on those scars and my hand in his side, I will not believe.'[3] Job's anguish appears even greater:

> I call to you, O God, but you never answer;
>   and when I pray, you pay no attention.
> You are treating me cruelly;
>   you persecute me with all your power.

You let the wind blow me away;
    you toss me about in a raging storm . . .
Why do you attack a ruined man,
    one who can do nothing but beg for pity?[4]

And yet while Job doesn't get an answer to his question he is
enfolded in the bigger questions when God puts to him,

Who are you to question my wisdom
    with your ignorant, empty words? . . .
Were you there when I made the world?[5]

Thomas, on the other hand, receives a straight answer: '. . .Thomas,
put your finger here, and look at my hands; then stretch out your
hand and put it in my side. Stop your doubting, and believe!'[6] Both
Thomas and Job are satisfied by the response of God. To one an
answer is given; to the other, bigger questions are posed. In both
answer and questions God is revealed.

When we confront the questions that go to the very core of our
faith and will not go away we inevitably find ourselves at a crossroads. Put very simply, stretched out before us are three options.
Option one is *dogmatism*, where we reinforce our faith stance from
any doubt by shoring it up with points of evidence and appealing
to external authorities or learned figures. Metaphorically, we dig
our heels in and ignore any evidence to the contrary as we hold on
to our faith, believing what we always have believed despite the
emptiness or shallowness these beliefs now convey. Far too often
this is the road to growing inner resentment and a closing down to
much of the reality of life. It is also often the path continuously
chosen, question after question, by the most vocal stalwarts of
faith in EPC churches. Having chosen not to explore their own
questions, they remain the most unwilling to allow the questions of
others to be heard.

The second option is a form of *reactionism* where the power of
doubt and the lack of answers take over and the tenets of faith are
cynically withdrawn from. People who had grown up in churches
and may once have believed in God, in an orthodox Christian
sense, now reject such a belief, taking on a new fundamentalism
regarding their new non-theism which can now often be held to as
strongly and rigidly as the Christian fundamentalists they ridicule.

The options for dogmatism or reactionism represent two polar extremes. There is, however, a third option. It is the decision not to retreat to simple answers (dogmatism) or non-answers (cynical withdrawal) but to live with the discomfort and the tensions of not knowing. In this direction lie gateways to the wonder of mystery and a paradoxical faith. It is the way of Ricoeur's second or willed naïveté. It is the way of mystery. A mystery that holds powerful seemingly opposite truths together.

This is what Nicholas of Cusa (1401–64) points to in his greatest work *De Docta Ignorantia*. Here he developed the idea of God as the *coincidentia oppositorum* – the coincidence of opposites – in which God is seen as the being where all opposites and contradictions meet and are reconciled. Carl Jung adapted this idea in many of his psychological writings on religion, altering the term to the *coniunctio oppositorum* – the conjunction of opposites.[7]

I have been going to the same spiritual director for six years. He has been an ordained Catholic priest for 40 years. I have come to respect him greatly as a man of faith and huge insight. He has said to me more than once that we all face our own set of doubts and in them people of faith often seem to follow one of two paths. Either they become 'rule-keepers' or 'people of mystery'.

My struggle with his advice has been twofold. First, accepting the fluidity of the world of mystery when I would so often like something more concrete to hang on to; and second, accepting the implication of becoming a person of mystery. In the Church it is the 'rule-keepers' who are most often respected and esteemed within the structures. People of mystery are more likely to be sidelined than those who keep to the old answers and formulas of the Church. In other words, there is always the cost of being misunderstood and not fitting in when you leave open the power of the questions.

Brenda put the same three options down in her journal like this:

Brenda The last three years have been a time of questioning most of my faith, and discarding the 'surface obsolete' in order to discover the essence of who I found God to be, and what my life response is to the truth I discover. This process formally began with a new journal: My aim and, I guess, purpose for writing this journal is to come out the other side of this phase of life in one of three places.

1   To be convinced of God, his person, his existence, his involvement in human life, and to be growing into a deeper knowledge of him and his ways, the result being that every part of my life would exist as a result of this knowledge, every choice, action, priority founded in God, whoever I find him to be.

2   To have discovered truth in another area, to find life and spirituality from a source that convinces me of its authenticity, and in doing so convicts me to devote myself and my life to the truth I find within it.

3   To be satisfied and content that there is no greater power than the human spirit, and to therefore enjoy life for what it presents itself to be, to make the most of the time I have here, and re-establish my priorities for my time here according to the resulting principles I discover.

It takes courage to write this down and to own it as the point we are at. It takes real courage to face the possibilities laid out and not to try to attach ourselves to either one before we even begin the journey of doubt. As T. A. Veling, a writer on faith in the post-modern context, puts it: 'There are times when we need to lose our way in order to be brought to a place of lostness, where the question can emerge, it is not this lostness itself that sustains us, rather, it serves to point us in a new direction, to find another way.'[8] But finding this new direction, this other way, often necessitates lost time. We intuitively know this when it comes to making important decisions:

> It is rarely the case that an important decision is made in an instant, or even overnight. Rather, we engage in a process of decision-making . . . such a process is often painful and we describe ourselves as agonising over the decision. What in fact we are often describing is the state of not knowing. This is a kind of in-between time when we know a decision has to be made, but it is not actually made . . . instinctively you know that staying in this chaotic in-between place, the place of boundary, is a vital part of the process. This is where the real discernment takes place.[9]

It is the same with the probing, irreconcilable questions of faith, where faith and doubt are not seen as the antithesis of each other, but are the two sides of the same coin. Often greater doubt precipitates greater faith. Maybe it is certainty, not doubt, that is the antithesis of faith.

Such questions lead to a wrestling with possible ways forward and a struggle for truth. 'Most of us', Kathleen Norris suggests, 'have had family members, friends and even enemies who have wrestled with us through important questions, who have helped us grow up, building something good out of the ruins we have made for ourselves.'[10] So too Israel, whose name means 'the one who contends, or who wrestles with God'. We sometimes need to be reminded that to be called Israel – the one who wrestles with God – was a title of endearment and praise from God.

In many evangelical circles it seems there is an unnecessary fear of questions. The fear appears to be that if we leave a question unanswered, people might head off in the wrong direction. Yet it is often only when we are free to make a choice that we are able to do so. Only when we have real choice are we able to fully choose the best. It is when we are not given choice that we are most likely to rebel.

Entering the realm of doubt and questions means entering a very vast expanse: an expanse that God invites Job into. God only answered his questions with bigger questions, but in so doing God had spoken to him personally and Job was free to move on with a new trust and his unanswered questions. For God's answer was pointing Job to the kind of reality a recent newspaper article raised when it described the vastness of space as seen through the travels of one of the first unmanned spacecraft:

> Pioneer Ten is the first man-made object to venture beyond our solar system. Launched on March the 2nd 1972 the last signal from the space craft was received on the 22nd of January 2003; it was then 12.2 billion kilometres from earth. Although all communication with earth has now been lost the spacecraft continues to coast toward the star Aldebaran in the constellation Taurus. It will take 2 million years to reach it.[11]

This statement dwarfs our life, our existence and our questions as they are set in a much larger context. It reminds us to:

Remember, as you read, and as you live,
nothing is ever simple.
Nothing,
The more it looks black and white,
The deeper you should dig
To find the grey.
Grey sounds dull,
But it is the colour of the mind.[12]

It is this thought that I took with me recently when I was invited to be a respondent at a day lecture series on the existence of God. The motivation for the day was the launching of a new book, *Christianity Without God*, by Professor Lloyd Geering. It follows a similar philosophy to that of Bishop Spong, the Jesus Seminar, and a host of other liberal non-theists. In this book, Geering questions the existence of God as a distinct being and, using a historical analysis of the biblical record, seeks to explain the emergence of the concept of God as a purely human construction: a construct that we in the modern world can now move away from.

My response was to try to learn from Job and point to bigger questions and ways of knowing that the postmodern world is reminding us of. I was particularly interested in what we can learn from looking at things from within, and thinking things together rather than thinking them apart. In the next few paragraphs I want to develop these two ways of thinking – not to provide answers for our questions but as examples of other ways of working with our questions. They are in effect two lenses of coming to an understanding of an issue that are not generally part of the discourse in EPC churches.

For example, in one part of *Christianity Without God* the author claims, 'It has never been at all clear how Jesus could be "perfect in Godhead" and also perfect in manhood, truly God and truly man at one and the same time.'[13] While appreciating the seeming inconsistency of these two attributes of God in the one sentence, they do seem to be inherent in the brilliance of the claim. If the nature of God were intelligible, definable and mathematically calculable it would lose all the mystery and all the layers of truthful understanding that the God–person paradox brings forth. This does not set up an irreconcilable dichotomy, but rather suggests that the juxtaposition of opposites can contain truth, profound truth, in a way that more reductionist approaches do not. The modern world's fascination for thinking things apart, which was the great strength of the modernist approach to learning, brings with it inherent dangers. Drawing on Parker Palmer's book *The Courage to Teach*, we need to remember that we can so easily reduce things down to this or that, plus or minus, on or off, black or white. When we do this, reality is fragmented into endless sets of either/or. It raises the question of what it would be like to think things together.

Niels Bohr, the Nobel Prize-winning physicist cited by Parker Palmer, says, 'The opposite of a true statement is a false statement, the opposite of a profound truth can be another profound truth.'[14] This leads us into the realm of paradox. Bohr argues that if we want to know what is essential we must stop thinking the world into pieces and start thinking it together again. Profound truth is the stuff of which paradoxes are made. To quote Parker Palmer,

> The poles of a paradox are like the poles of a battery: hold them together, and they generate the energy of life; pull them apart, and the current stops flowing. When we separate any of the profound paired truths of our lives, both poles become lifeless spectres of themselves – and we become lifeless as well.[15]

To rely on the reductionist approach of modern religious studies is to make it seem as if the person of Jesus, the mysteries and otherness of God, the wonders of the Trinity and the paradoxes of the scriptures are being placed on the operating table and dissected, blood vessel by blood vessel, nerve by nerve, organ by organ, until the life-blood has long since drained away. A process a bit like that of the American Civil War surgeon who, story has it, had men hold down a wounded soldier while he performed meticulous and extensive surgery, never finishing until the last stitch was perfectly completed – and long after the soldier had died.

On the other hand, thinking things together rather than thinking them apart in some sort of surgical way can lead to robust and truthful paradoxes. Parker Palmer introduces a second way of understanding when he suggests that we can understand something not simply by standing outside of it and observing it from the vantage point of seeming neutrality but also by standing within it, as it were, and considering it from within rather than without. In essence, this is what to 'understand' means – literally to stand under.

Palmer illustrates this using the work of the famous biologist Barbara McClintock. This Nobel Prize winner is one of the greatest biologists of modern times. In her work on the genetic makeup of corn plants she sought to understand the genetics of living organisms, not by removing them from their context and analysing them, but by deliberately observing how genes function in their environment rather than regarding them merely as isolated entities. It is not that she didn't engage in precise thinking and impeccable data collection and analysis; she went further than these skills as she gained valuable knowledge by empathizing with her corn plants, submerging herself in their world and dissolving the boundary between object and observer.[16] If this is true of genetic biology it is equally true in our understanding of spiritual mysteries. Standing outside and trying to be objective gives one perspective, but another equally important one is gained by standing within the faith and seeking to understand it from within its teachings, prayers, liturgies and worship.

The rational logic of pulling things apart, observing and analysing them from a distance without personal engagement certainly does bring us to conclusions, but on its own the conclusions drawn are at best incomplete. Pursuing a more paradoxical approach and way of knowing is messy and complex, and sometimes contradictory, as we live with the tension of opposites. But that tension can also, at times, pull us open to bigger possibilities and greater realities. It is the logic of parenting. Every parent knows the minefield of bringing up children, and the tensions, pain and struggles that this inevitably brings. Yet we also probably have experienced the way such tensions pull us open to larger and larger love for our kids.

When it comes to God and Christ, the Trinity and the scriptures, it is perhaps like understanding love. An intellectual dissection only takes you so far. Experiencing love, entering the reality of being loved and giving love to another means far more than any intellectual analysis from the sidelines. In doing so we enter the *mysterium tremendum*: that tremendous mystery of God in which we realize that the substance of God's silence can often ground us more deeply than the superficiality of any answer we may want to throw at our questions. For as our questions grow, so too can our perception of God. Remember the scene in Narnia when Lucy finally found Aslan for the second time years after their first meeting:

'Aslan, Aslan. Dear Aslan,' sobbed Lucy. 'At last.'

The great beast rolled over on his side so that Lucy fell, half sitting and half lying between his front paws. He bent forward and just touched her nose with his tongue. His warm breath came all round her. She gazed up into the large wise face.

'Welcome, child,' he said.

'Aslan,' said Lucy. 'You're bigger.'

'That is because you are older, little one,' answered he.

'Not because you are?'

'I am not. But every year you grow, you will find me bigger,' said Aslan.[17]

Through this picture C. S. Lewis invites us to see God in new ways. It is this kind of understanding that Brenda came to as she wrestled with her own questions about God, faith, scripture and what it means to follow God in life.

> *Brenda* I still have many questions. But I have discovered something of the beauty of mystery, of things that are 'too wonderful for me, too lofty for me to attain'. I feel that my spiritual journey was one that required me to die on the inside in order to truly come alive to God, a God that was a lot bigger than I'd ever imagined, giving me a new understanding of the verse: 'Unless a seed falls to the ground and dies it can bear no fruit.'

And as we wrestle with our own questions, the following words of St John of the Cross may be worth holding on to:

> To come to what you know not
> You must go by the way where you know not . . .
> To come to what you are not
> You must go by a way where you are not.[18]

5

Truth In and Beyond Myth

————◄◦►————

People would rather have the security of false truth than the freedom of ambiguous reality.

(Eric Fromm)[1]

William We had got to the point where we had thrown so much out, we didn't believe it any longer, we just didn't know and we didn't have any interest in knowing. I am still going through the 'I don't want to read my Bible' bit. I still need longer to put a lot of those ways of seeing it – and what it says – behind me. I am starting to get glimpses and someone will talk about a phrase from the Bible and I think, yes, it fits in nicely and it works. I'm still not at the point where I can pick up my Bible and read it again. We just had to have a period of rest without even thinking about these sorts of things. And that is probably what happened over the first few years, we just didn't want to think about those things at all – we just wanted to get on with everything else in our lives.

In the quote above, William describes his and Jennifer's feelings about the Bible. Their church, and William and Jennifer themselves, have for many years held to the Bible as at least 'the inspired word of God', if not as 'the inerrant word of God'. The scriptures have been the foundation of their lives and faith for a long time. Although for William, and many others, past belief and usage of the Bible is not up for question, this surety has crumbled for them as new, insistent questions, doubts and experiences have been encountered. What used to be so clear and reliable has now become far more problematic. For each of us the questions are different, and they arise with new urgency from quite different sources.

Russell I started to question . . . I started getting into eschatology and realized there were lots of ways of understanding the end times. But I had grown up on a diet of the truth. This has always been a key theme in my life: what is the truth? I became saved because this is the truth.

It was only as I started to get older that it started to dawn on me that there was this very problematic issue of what is the truth. Because it is defined by somebody and given or taught and therefore is open to evaluation. There were some things . . . this is a bit more personal, but I remember this is the first thing I had ever started to question – the morality surrounding masturbation. To put it in context, that was seen as a very heavy sin. Have you read Foucault? He says if we deny these aspects they will nevertheless reoccur in our discourse. So we can never eliminate these things – they just reoccur. When I think of my Christian community there was so much talk about sex. But it was done in such a way – and I remember doing this myself; especially the masturbation thing – that it was wrong. It was the first thing I really started to question. That was the start for me . . . there were certainly people there with divergent views, but they just kept quiet. For me it was a big issue because truth was truth. But there was nevertheless a dominant discourse, and it would take a dominant person to stand against that.

When this happens people often do what Russell and William have done. They put the Bible down because they could no longer read it as the word of God in the way they used to, and at this point they have no other way of interpreting it. When this happens it can so easily be discarded. Another way of assessing the scriptures and new lenses through which to see them are now needed because the old ways are no longer sufficient. Without such a changed perspective the Bible is often simply left. Before a new lens or perspective on scripture can be considered many people have to put down their old ways. To quote the American pastor Mary Tuomi Hammond again, we have to 'decontaminate the Bible' before we can approach with fresh eyes.[2]

This is a common story among many of the church leavers I have spent time with, and one that is not easily resolved. We need to remember that it takes genuine courage and internal conviction to come to this point. As Eric Fromm[3] said, many 'people would rather have the security of false truth than the freedom of ambiguous reality'. Alan Jones takes the implications of this crossroad further:

> Ask Christian believers what they would do if they had to choose between Jesus Christ and the Truth. There are easy ways to slip out from underneath this question, 'since Christ is the Truth, I don't see any conflict.' But the way of believing that I espouse would always choose the Truth (even if one's perception of it turned out to be wrong) and allow the false object of faith to dissolve. I do not pretend that this is easy; but I can bear witness to the fact that when I have made the choice, a fresh and living 'Christ' appears. There is an epiphany.[4]

This chapter is for those who are willing to set down their previous understandings of scripture and to consider new lenses through which to understand the collected writings we call the Bible. The lens I want to suggest is the lens of myth.

If you were to ask any group of Christians today who the greatest Christian apologist of the last century was you would no doubt be given the name C. S. Lewis. Yet I wonder if the same people realize how this rational defender of the faith came to be a Christian. A major factor in his decision was his long friendship with J. R. R. Tolkien. Lewis found it very difficult to accept that this good friend who was 'one of the most interesting, intellectual and intelligent men he had ever met' was a devout Christian.[5] Over more than a five-year period the two academics of ancient mythologies and legends met together and talked about many things, including Tolkien's faith in God. In September 1931 Tolkien, Lewis and another friend had dinner together and then went for a stroll. As they walked, the conversation turned to Christian faith. Lewis, although accepting some form of God, could not accept that the story of Jesus coming to earth in order to die on the cross and save humanity was anything but myth.

To Lewis 'the story of Christ was simply just another legend, another myth no more accurate or meaningful to him and the modern world than any other'. And at their root, he believed, myths are of course, lies.[6] Tolkien apparently listened to Lewis's argument and watched as Lewis threw his hands in the air at the conclusion of his statement and said, 'so, how then can you believe the Christ story to be anything but an ancient legend?'.[7] Tolkien came back with an argument that would change Lewis' life. What he said was 'myths are most certainly not lies. Myths derive from a kernel of truth and portray very specific cultural meaning .'[8] If Christianity was based on what Lewis considered the myth of Christ, then, Tolkien argued 'call it a myth if you like, but it was constructed upon real events and it was inspired by a deep truth'. Tolkien believed this 'myth' provided a route, an 'in-road', to a deeper spiritual truth.

Although Lewis was not immediately convinced and many other factors were involved, he later wrote to a friend saying he had moved in his convictions and now fully embraced Christ. 'The idea that Christianity was a true myth',[9] the idea planted by the comments of Tolkien, was to be 'the heart of what Lewis spent the rest of his literary career describing'.[10]

What Tolkien offered was another way through the intellectual impasse about the Bible. In evangelical circles, born as they are from the early forms of fundamentalism in the twentieth century, any attack on the scriptures as anything but truth is met with dog-matisms and endless arguments. Often, though, such attempts to validate the 'truth' of the scriptures carry little weight as they fall into the very pothole that many people are trying to avoid. This is the pothole that claims we have the ability to prove what is true or false. The pothole is a legacy from the modernist approach to the world in which rational scientists, theologians and historians were seen as being able to 'prove' the veracity of all sorts of things. What many postmoderns seek today is not simply a modernist set of proofs, however compelling, but an entering into truth that is far deeper and more profound than the sort of data gained from his-torical analysis or microscopic investigation. They seek the sort of truth that can look at the scriptures and say, 'Yes, these are human constructs written by people every bit as fallible and human as ourselves.' They reflect the cultural context in which they were written and they at least appear on the surface to carry contradic-tory statements and errors, *but* they also convey profound truth that has shaped millions of lives and given courage to generations. They describe the best of human values, relationships and living, and they speak of God, 'the Other', as a being who both created all that is and is connected to all that is in ways that are loving, personal, caring and determinative. In other words, within these words – human words – something else is at work. They can be seen as 'myths' in the sense that Tolkien does but they must be seen not as the myths we equate with lies and children's fables but with the 'myths' that convey truth, are inspired by deeper truth and provide 'an in-road to a deeper spiritual truth'.

Andrew Newberg and Eugene D'Aquili, in their fascinating book *Why God Won't Go Away: Brain Science and the Biology of Belief*, state that:

> Contrary to the meaning conveyed by modern usage, the term *myth* is not a synonym for 'fantasy' or 'fable'. It does not specifically imply falsehood or fabrication. Instead, in its classical definition, the word has an older, deeper meaning. It comes from the Greek *mythos*, which translates as 'word', but one spoken with deep, unquestioned authority. *Mythos* is, in turn, anchored in the Greek term *musteion*, which, according to religion scholar Karen Armstrong, author of *A History of God*, means 'to close the eyes or the mouth', rooting myth, Armstrong says, 'in an experience of darkness and silence'.[11]

Newberg and D'Aquili, drawing on the work of Joseph Campbell, go on to argue that myths show us

> what is most important, and what, in terms of the inner life, is most deeply and profoundly true. The power of myth lies beneath its literal interpretations, in the ability of its universal symbols and themes to connect us with the most essential parts of ourselves in ways that logic and reason alone cannot . . . In this sense, the story of Jesus is a myth even if it were literally and historically true.[12]

Understanding myths in this way means that two equally unhelpful approaches can be transcended when it comes to how we view the scriptures. First, the approach that sees every word and verse as somehow the divine products of God – infallible, unchangeable, and beyond human investigation and critique; and second, the equally unhelpful approach that sees the whole scripture as simply a human record of a past culture, world view and belief. Both are ultimately unhelpful. Yet, as Tolkien pointed out, they can be transcended by a third alternative approach in which we see the scriptures as human constructs, but human constructs that have and continue to convey profound truth about being human, about the purpose and meaning of life, and, most significantly, about the ultimate being we call God.

To approach the scriptures as myths in this way, 'myths' in the Tolkien sense, is to demythologize them: to see them not as 'lies' or 'fables and fantasy' in the way that 'myths' are so often viewed but as conveyors of profound and essential truth. Let me illustrate.

Last Christmas there were three stories vying for the attention and patronage of people across the world. The first was the story of a vulnerable boy brought up in an ordinary family by normal, even uninspiring, parents. Yet he is no ordinary child; rather he is seen from an early age as one who carries the mark: a mark that identifies him as supernatural. Later, as a young boy, he bursts on to the public scene and is involved in the fight of good over evil, in protecting truth and life from the powers who want to use every-thing for their own evil purposes and selfish gain. This is the story of Harry Potter, Ron, Hermione, the good angel Hagrid, Professor Dumbledore and the evil power Voldemort.

The second story clamouring for our patronage was originally written by J. R. R. Tolkien and has recently been made into a film. In some ways it is a very similar story to that of Harry Potter. Again the pursuit of good against evil, truth over lies and the need for courage and a long journey in the pursuit of all that is true and good. In this story Professor Dumbledore is replaced by Gandalf, Harry by Frodo, Hogwarts School by Middle Earth and the philosopher's stone by the power of the ring.

Our third and final story is again that of a boy born to ordinary, unspectacular parents. A person who is called to do much in the war between good and evil, truth and falsehood. He, like Harry and Frodo, must risk all to show truth, gain life for others and point out a better way of living. He too is opposed by the forces of evil and his life too is at risk as his enemies plot against him. This final story is the story of Jesus. The story that takes us from cradle to cross, from Bethlehem to Jerusalem, from the carpenter's questions to the mysteries of God.

These three stories were all vying for our attention and alle-giance last Christmas. How do we differentiate between them? Which is 'true' and which is 'myth'? This is an important question and one which can be answered a number of different ways. The most obvious is through an attempt to peel back the layers to find the historical facts (truth) within the story. Another possibility is to look at the origins of the stories. What 'truth' inspired each of them to be written? A third method would be to look at the truth they carry or convey, and a final approach might be to look at the impact they have on the life of a listener; in other words, their consequential truth. Let us use these criteria to assess the three stories.

While the Harry Potter stories do not reveal factual truth, they were inspired (according to some commentators) by J. K. Rowling's interest in the *Lord of the Rings*. Like the Harry Potter stories, the *Lord of the Rings* trilogy does not claim to be factually true but it was inspired by very factual events. These factual events were Tolkien's life and his Christian faith. The final story, the Jesus story, is much like the others in many ways. However, the biblical record claims that this story is real or true in other senses.

Looking at the account of Jesus' birth drawn from Luke's Gospel we read the claim that these events happened in history. Luke speaks specifically of Caesar Augustus and Quirinius, Governor of Syria. These are characters of recorded history who lived and had their influence in real time. Unlike Harry and Frodo, the birth of Jesus claims not simply to be a timeless story but a story that occurred in real time.

The Luke account does not just locate Jesus in time but also in space, as Luke describes events not in Middle Earth, or via platform nine and three-quarters but in locatable towns and regions of Galilee and Bethlehem that we can find on the map, go and visit, or read about; places which are known through archaeology, pottery and writings of the period.

The Luke story is not only located in time and space but it is also located in people whose family line we know. These aren't strange people brought in on a flying motorbike, or half people who are somehow related to humans but also quite distinct. No, this is about the family of Joseph a carpenter, who was from the line of David whose family tree could be traced and whose ancestors are known; and Mary, a young maid. The Luke story claims to be true in ways that the Harry Potter story and the *Lord of the Rings* do not.

So which is true and which is myth? All three convey truth and may be seen as good psychology, as archetypal stories that are 'true' because they are stories that relate to us all, that call forth the good, the honest and the courageous in all of us and ask us to risk in pursuit of life and hope and truth. Two of the stories – *Lord of the Rings* and the Jesus story – are inspired by events that happened in the real lives of people. One, however, goes further still. It claims to be true factually: that is, to speak of historical events that happened at a certain time and place and with known people. For some people this 'factual truth' will be very important; for others, it is of less significance. For both, the story can convey and inspire truthful living. Whether this 'factual truth' is personally significant to us or not, the fact that the Jesus story is different from the Harry and Frodo stories is also seen in one other crucial sense. That is, the inherent claims of the story do not just encourage us to pursue truth, but that truth itself is found in the central character of the story – Jesus Christ. Not just that we should fight for good, but that all good is found and sourced in God. Not just that we should live loving lives, but the model and source of all love is God. Not just that we should pursue life and live fully, but that all life is sourced in God. This story doesn't simply encourage us to pursue these greater goals, but also tells us where they are to be found and from whom they came. In other words, these are not just inspired stories or simply factual events but an account of a God who is deeply connected to the world and to each one of us: a God who wants to connect with us in deep and profound ways to help us in the pursuit of being our whole selves, which is our true and holy self.

In the end it is this final sense of truthfulness that the scriptures convey which is of paramount importance. That is their ontological, core or essential truth. The scriptural stories are good stories, but they are also more: they are stories which convey God in a way no other story can. It is this essential core – the account of God in Christ – that is the substance of Christian faith. For faith must have substance. Faith is not a reality itself but profound trust in something. Faith in faith is as barren as being in love with love rather than being in love with a person, place or project. Faith in faith is like having money that you spend only on the accumulation of more money. So too, Christian faith is ultimately faith in God and God's truth. Professor Kuitert describes it thus:

The statement 'the Bible is the word of God inspired by the Spirit' is of precisely the same order as 'Jesus is God's Son' or 'God is gracious and merciful'. It can't both be a statement of faith and at the same time a foundation for one. The Bible isn't the firm ground on which faith is anchored: the firm ground is God.[13]

God's truth is a truth that can be apprehended in many forms, including through a number of ways of understanding scripture. Let us end this chapter by listening to the journey Brenda moved through as she grappled with how to understand the Bible.

Brenda Scripture has been a battlefield all its own. My journey has come through the years of absolutely soaking in scripture, memorizing as much as I could, applying scripture to every situation I faced, using it as an answer book for every dilemma, and expecting God to speak to me through it every time it 'magically' opened.

Then I entered a place where I found scripture incredibly painful. Most of it, for a long time, made little sense to me; if anything, it repelled me. I battled with scriptural concepts and portrayals of judgement, of salvation, of gender, of God's intervention, of suffering, of power and its misuse, of contradiction, of arrogance and control, of only one truth. For a long time I could not read passages of scripture without real distress. One verse in a psalm did, however, make perfect sense of my experience – 'Deep calls to deep in the roar of your waterfalls . . . all your waves and breakers crash and crush me.' I felt like I was being crushed in a sea of 'spiritual truths' that were too big for me to bear.

To some of the scriptural dilemmas I have found answers – mostly through fresh interpretations, language explanations and expanded possibilities. But there are still a decent number that continue to confound me . . . an interesting phenomenon, however, is that the wrestle itself has left me knowing, like Jacob, that I have somehow connected with the Almighty in a way that I could never have done without it. In some ways I feel I bear the limp, in other ways my soul is more alive to God than ever.

More recently scripture has become a historical masterpiece, and a precious tool for communication with the Supreme Being and for gaining wisdom. But not in the way I used to think it would make me wise. I am finding that the wisdom of scripture is acquired not by memorizing its message, or directly applying a + b = c, but wisdom grows through the often painful integration of scripture's principles with everyday life. God is indeed, in my perception, behind this book, but not as I may once have understood it.

6

Prayer In and Beyond Words

◄○►

The fruit of silence is prayer, the fruit of prayer
is faith, the fruit of faith is love, the fruit of love
is service, the fruit of service is peace.
(Mother Teresa)[1]

For some people the issues of truth and meaning are far less pressing than the sense of a deeper personal reality to their faith; the knowledge that they are deeply connecting with God. This was the case for Jamie who was converted as a young adult, became deeply involved in a Pentecostal church for many years, then went overseas to do mission work. He has subsequently come home, completed a doctorate and is now leading a significant government rehabilitation programme:

Jamie Whenever I discuss with people that I'm no longer involved in church circles, to church associates they will always say that it's very difficult to hold Christian faith and pursue university education. But, you see, intellectually I have never had a problem with Christianity: as a philosophical, cosmological system it seems to me to be very coherent. There is nothing about it as a system that I struggle with. I struggle with the excesses of Pentecostal sort of teachings, super spiritual sort of stuff. But as for, you know, the basic tenets of the creator God, of redemption of Christ, all that stuff, I don't find anything there that isn't believable. Although one thing that does trouble me is the different religions and how they all think they are right. I've never really sorted that out. But nevertheless Christianity has always made good sense to me. That has never been the problem; I've never had trouble over that.

But my troubles always came out of a lack of some sort of inner sense of reality. The inward stuff. The sense of some sort of spirituality, of some sort of connecting with God, some sort of relationship – not just an idea. You see, that had always been the problem. I don't know why, I wouldn't have a clue, to be honest, why it is that I was unable to connect. So I gave up on that quest, and then what I was left with was just the system, the concepts, the ideas. And as time has gone by, it seemed to me 'Of what tangible use is it? What does it matter if I have this or that idea in my head?' I suppose since leaving the church I have gradually evolved to the position . . . where, in a way, I don't think about it, it just doesn't mean anything. People talk about spirituality and I feel envious, I wish I knew about that stuff; but I don't! And I'm not interested any more in talking to people as if it was meaningful. I don't experience this. Therefore I've got nothing to say. I'm not interested in it; no, that's not true. I still remain interested in it. If somebody can find some experience or someone can convince me of some new pathway through which I can achieve that kind of living, I think I would be very interested in it. I would really respond to that. But they would probably be up against a fair bit of cynicism – as a result of the years of being involved in church life and constantly being promised that this was what Christianity was all about.

Jamie is by no means unusual, as the journeys of the church leavers tracked over the last five years show, when it comes to prayer. Typically those who had returned to an EPC church, or maintained an EPC faith belief structure outside of a church involvement, talked about prayer as a means of communication with God, as being essential to Christian life and strongly focused on results and answers. In contrast, those, like Jamie, in the midst of the deconstruction of their own faith, talked of prayer as an 'occasional' experience, focusing less on asking for things in prayer and less as a connecting point with God.

> *Bronwyn* I hadn't realized how many 'asks' my prayer contained. I still pray from time to time but it's more for me to accept life in all its wholeness . . . I get a greater sense of how big this world is, how time, nature, changing theology is just part of the world and us.

Those who had moved into and to some extent through desert experiences came again to affirm the value of prayer as communication or contact with God. They indicated that they were both practising prayer more now as well as engaging in more reflection about the meaning of prayer for them personally. In so doing they talked in very personal language of prayer as an ongoing part of their daily lives:

Emma Prayer is a continuing conversation . . .

Jeremy Prayer is an attitude of life . . .

Michelle Prayer is listening, awareness, being open to life . . .

These people from the deserts of prayer spoke of a new and for them very strong thread in their understanding of prayer when they mentioned that prayer not only allows contact with God but enables their 'true self' to grow.

Rob Prayer is seeking to be moved into the place where I can truly be who I am.

Jeremy In prayer I'm in contact with my true self and fully aware of who I am.

Mark Prayer is more relationship building, say, than changing events through prayers . . . A sense of one-ness with God, being transported to another space. A remembering who I am and who God is.

Clearly these people's desert experiences have deeply affected their prayer: not just what they do when they pray but how they understand the dynamic of prayer and what prayer is all about for them. It is something Jamie hadn't yet found when I spoke with him. Many others do work through the times of questioning, doubting, failure, hopelessness and despair, and for them prayer is profoundly and irreversibly changed in the process. Somehow their prayer seems to move from a focus on the details of methodology and finding 'answers' to the simplicity of being with. This way of prayer is epitomized in a quote from Mother Teresa when she said 'the fruit of listening is prayer . . .' Prayer, therefore, is born in listening and is the response of deep listening. Listening to ourselves, others and the world.

Recently I asked Dr Peter Millar about prayer. Peter, a Scottish writer and activist, is a former warden of Iona Abbey and a member of the Iona Community. Over the last 30 years Peter and his late wife Dorothy have been involved in various parts of the world with marginal people and have campaigned ceaselessly for global justice. Many of his books reflect this radical Christian spirituality of engagement with the modern world and the life of prayer. When I asked him about prayer he replied:

> In my own life prayer is both about speaking words and listening. By that I mean that there are various dimensions in the life of prayer which is not for me a disconnected experience but integral to the ups and downs of everyday living. Prayer is earthed in the heart and soul rather than in the mind – a truth which does not imply that we should not reflect on the nature of prayer and on the words that we use. As a member of the Iona Community my spiritual life is to a certain extent framed in prayer which is a central part of the community's rule. But prayer is not a detached experience, for I believe that our lives are also prayers – we carry prayer within all our daily activities. Prayer and ordinary living are never disconnected. In the Gospels we are given some basic models of praying and it is often the very simple prayers rooted in an authentic life which are the most powerful.

Peter's reply raises interesting themes: What does it mean to have a life framed by prayer? How is prayer connected to the daily ups and downs of life? In what ways are our lives also prayers? But perhaps most positively, his final statement that very simple prayers rooted in an authentic life are often the most powerful.

These comments stand in stark contrast to the prayer encouraged in many Christian circles, especially EPC church circles. Here the models of prayer are often very wordy and full of clichés and Christian code. They can be so disconnected from the rest of our lives and our deepest feelings and passions that they are, to put it frankly, boring. I remember on more than one occasion sitting down to pray and finding some time into my 'wordy' prayers that I wasn't listening. And if I wasn't listening why should I expect that God would? The prayer had the 'right' words in it but it didn't mean anything to me, it wasn't drawn from deep within me – I wasn't being honest. Luther would remind us at such times that 'the curses of a godless man can sound more pleasant in God's ears than the hallelujahs of the pious'.

We have said repeatedly that going through desert experiences of faith or, as St John of the Cross called these times, dark nights of the soul, means being stripped of the unnecessary. This is true in prayer as well. We cannot be called into new ways until we set down the old. Patterns of praying that don't work are shown to be empty when the heat is really on, and not surprisingly they have to be discarded: sometimes with a great deal of anger and frustration about the sense of being sold a dud.

Perhaps we need to start with a fresh page – prayer, as Clement of Alexandria wrote, is keeping company with God.[2] Thomas à Kempis called prayer 'a familiar friendship with Jesus'. It is about a deepening relationship of friendship and openness. Not methods, results or even feelings.

One of the most well-known images of prayer is Albrecht Dürer's famous etching of the praying hands. The story behind this picture began around 1490 with two young struggling artists who were either brothers or close friends. Both were very poor and had to work to support themselves and could only train as artists in their spare time. In order to earn an income they both worked in the nearby mines or quarries. As time went on they realized that if they kept going as they were, neither of them would make it to be an artist. So they decided to toss a coin and the winner would go off to art school while the other would carry on working in the mines to earn the money for the first's tuition. The hope was that once one was trained he could then support the other through the sale of his art. Albrecht won and went off to art school. Some years later, when his training was completed and he had become a successful artist, he returned to his home town so that his friend Franz could go to art school. Coming back, he found Franz's hands had been ruined from the manual work. His fingers had been broken and not re-set properly and arthritis was setting in. Franz would never be an artist. One day Albrecht found Franz on his knees, hands clasped in prayer, gnarled and yet offered to God. Albrecht quickly sketched his hands showing how deeply friendship and prayer are so intimately linked.[3]

Prayer is the language of friendship – the language of love. Prayer, I think, is very much like kissing. On a more humorous level there are the obvious similarities, like being unsure whether to leave our eyes open or shut, whether to go 'um' or 'mmh' and make other encouraging noises. In both there is the vexed issue of tongues. Yet on a more serious level they are both languages of love and intimacy. They both signal a special, personal and unique relationship. In both we feel very awkward as we begin – perhaps even embarrassed. Both take a long time for us to learn how to be in tune with our partner. They are both personal and somewhat embarrassing to try to explain at a personal level, and they are both splendidly useless in the sense that they don't appear to achieve anything. In fact, because they are languages of love, it would be mercenary to suggest that they are entered into as a means/ends equation.

The link between prayer and kissing is not simply humorous or illustrative but also deeply biblical and revelatory. The biblical accounts of kissing are perhaps more extensive and more revealing about our relationship with God than we might first have expected. There are the well-known examples of Judas betraying Jesus with a kiss and Mary Magdalene kissing Jesus' feet. But there are also the less familiar: the father kissing the prodigal son as he returns; Jesus saying to Peter, 'You never kissed me as she did',[4] Paul being showered in kisses by the elders at Ephesus, and church members being told to greet each other with a kiss.[5] Some clearly followed this instruction to such an extent that Clement of Alexandria complained there was too much of it going on. The biblical use of the image of the kiss is highly revelatory. In Jewish tradition Moses, Enoch and Elijah were taken into heaven by the kiss of God, and eternity itself was seen as the perfect kiss that flows from God. So too, human life was kissed into being as God breathed into humans the breath of life and the Holy Spirit was given to the early Church as Jesus did the same thing, breathing the Holy Spirit into the disciples. Now if the gift of human life, the coming of the Spirit and eternity are seen as the kiss of God, then surely the link between kissing and our relationship with God in prayer is worthy of some greater reflection.

The languages of love, prayer and kissing help us to see the intimacy and personal and loving nature of prayer.

The scriptures begin with a remarkable picture of the relationship between God and the people in the garden. Genesis 3.8 reminds us that the Lord God walked in the garden to meet with the man and the woman in the cool of the evening. In the imagery of the text we see God finishing his work in the realm of good and evil, and at the end of the day entering the protected environment of the man and the woman in order to spend the cool of the evening with them. This image is highly relational, intimate and warm. Many of us have enjoyed a long chat with others at the end of the day as the evening slowly turns to night. Such conversations are not forced or formal – simply relaxed and relational. The kind of natural friendship that Liz longs for:

> *Liz* Prayer I think is important too, but I suppose I would like to see prayer more as a way of life than something that I would necessarily do for ten minutes a day. It's more a sense of relationship. A sense of communion with God, that goes with me throughout my waking hours rather than something I just did for a few minutes now and then.

The story of God in the garden with the man and the woman in the evening tells us more about prayer as well. As we read on through the story we see that the Lord God called out to the man and the woman but they hid. When the Lord God called out to them asking why they were hiding the man replied, 'I heard you in the garden and I was afraid because I was naked, so I hid.' Because he was afraid he didn't want to meet with God, and he was afraid because he was naked and vulnerable. He didn't want to be exposed to God, to be seen for who he really was. Whether we say the words of prayer or not, we can also hide from God. For some hide by not praying while others hide by saying lots of words and never letting their true selves be exposed before God. In both cases it begs the question as to what we are afraid of.

Why don't we head back to the garden and find God? Dominant in our set of reasons not to do so is often fear. We too are afraid and the fear traps us. Is it fear of God not being there? Fear of being unanswered? Fear of who God really is? Or fear of what God might do with us? Clearly our image of God has changed as our faith has crumbled under the weight of questions, grief, pain, despair and failure. Now unsure of who it is we are approaching, we fearfully wait on the sidelines of prayer. For some, resentment also holds us on the sidelines. God has let us down and we fear it will happen again. Our present alienation from God is the result of the ever-present shadow of a previous let-down. An unanswered prayer or undeserved disaster breeds resentment for God: a resentment which can continue on as an open wound that never heals. Raw and open, we constantly return to pick at it, removing any potentially healing scabs as we recall the hurt with ghoulish pleasure. Time and the years only make such wounds worsen, causing infections to spread and our sense of hurt to deepen. It takes courage to face God in our fear and vulnerability and with our resentments and hurts. Again and again these are the beginning points of the psalms – the prayer book of scripture. The cry of David from two of the psalms conveys the pain:

> My God, my God, why have you deserted me?
>   Why are you so far away?
> Won't you listen to my groans
>   and come to my rescue?
> I cry out day and night,
> but you don't answer,
>   and I can never rest.[6]

> Yahweh, don't shut me out;
> don't give me the silent treatment, O God.[7]

These are the upfront and honest prayers of a struggler caught in fear, the silence of God and personal resentment. Without hiding his true self he comes asking whether it is safe to approach God. Like Susan who asks anxiously about Aslan the figure of God in C. S. Lewis' Narnia stories:

'I shall feel nervous about meeting a lion.'
    'That you will, dearie, and no mistake,' said Mrs Beaver, 'if there's anyone who can appear before Aslan without their knees knocking, they're either braver than most or else just silly.'
    'Then He isn't safe?' said Lucy.
    'Safe' said Mr Beaver . . . ''Course He isn't safe. But He's good.'[8]

Adam wanted to cover up, to hide the reality of his inner feelings and thoughts. In this sense we are often so like Adam, either trying to cover up before we go near God with ill-fitting clothes or trying to flee God's presence altogether. Covering up or fleeing leads us further and further away from a genuine encounter with God and our own inner reality. It is time, in the words of the old hymn, to ask 'from unreality set us free'. So that we can walk in the garden and encounter there again the presence of God.

The fact that this meeting with God in the Genesis story occurs in a garden is significant. It is linked to the New Testament instruction of Jesus to 'consider the lilies of the field'. Listening to the waves and wind, seeing the ocean in its various moods, observing the flight of a bird or laughing at the antics of a kitten can all be fuel for prayer. This is the kind of prayer that shares the wonders of creation with our creator. It is the slow process of learning to listen to and see nature and then sharing what we see and hear with God. The fruit of such listening and watching is, as Mother Teresa said, prayer. Listening and watching the physical environment provides a rich library of prayers: the fodder of our prayers and the conveyors of God's word to us. Reconnections in prayer can so often begin in nature; gently and fully aware of all that holds us back, we stop hiding and running to listen and watch. But this is most often learnt slowly and often with help.

A friend describes his own experience of this as his faith is slowly being reshaped:

> *Ray* I find myself deeply moved and fortified by very simple and mundane things. I was recently in a Redwood forest and found myself crying in delight at the magnificence of it all. At other times I catch myself smiling as I watch our cat stretched out in simple enjoyment or in cute mode in front of the fire. Our nephews and nieces are good to be with . . . I find myself celebrating the materiality of life – things like the physicality of the environment, autumn colours, flowers, plants and growing vegetables, smells and sounds, the impact of beautiful things, art and architecture, good coffee, chocolate and a glass of wine, animals and their companionship, and books. I call these sacramental experiences. They convey to me a sense of God's goodness and creativity, and remind me of the responsibilities given to us for their use and care.

Ray, like many, found the guidance of a spiritual director very helpful as he tentatively opened himself to God in these new ways. When we began in prayer we didn't need the guidance and reassurance of a companion, but now with our naïve faith in tatters we do need someone else to be with us, offering their insights and support. But this can't just be anyone. We are not called to share our pearls with swine but with those who have journeyed far with God and remain journeyers themselves in the life of prayer.

Our beginnings are often quite short and simple. Like a pre-schooler's picture – simple and messy. But in the eyes of a parent the child can never draw a bad picture. So too our prayers, born from honesty, hiding nothing, may be simple, even clumsy; but they are, every single one of them, loved by God. And over time child and prayer, reinforced by the acceptance of parent or God, are able to move from stick people and messy shading into richer detail, more precision and a greater clarity.

Over time we can begin to move from listening to nature to listening to our own inner selves, our inner truth or to unpacking our dreams and the messages they convey. From here we may begin to listen again to the words of scripture or the pain and struggles of the world and bring the fruit of these listenings to our prayer as well: slowly, cautiously, gently beginning to be befriended by God while offering God our friendship and companionship.

Perhaps the greatest of the teachers of prayer since the days of Christ was St John of the Cross. John, as we saw in Chapter 3, was a man of great suffering and wonderful insight. Imprisoned in a stuffy hole in the ground, encompassed in darkness, stillness and silence, John faced the worst of all punishments: absolute solitude coupled with the fear of the ever-present prospect of torture and death. Surely, if God has deserted anyone since that cry of Christ on the cross, it was John locked in this cistern of darkness and sewage.

Yet it was here in the darkness and squalor that John finds God. He states that finding God is like sitting in a dark room on one's own. Then after some time we realize we are not alone. There is someone else in the room. He has always been there and his silhouette is slowly becoming clearer. 'There in the midst of obscurity, the presence, imperceptible, dark and gentle.' John's advice was that many journeyers reach this point of inversion but few pass beyond it. Why? Because fear stops us from going further. The same fear that stops us from trusting God as he leads us into the foolishness of God. Fear of God's transforming light in the midst of our own personal darkness. But, John advises, the night is there to remind us that God is taking us somewhere, that he takes us there in darkness, and to go with him requires faith. In the darkness we cannot rely on our senses to lead us and must relinquish ourselves into the care of God's Spirit. Nor can we end the darkness and make the daylight come. We cannot stop the night or hasten the day. It is, as John describes it, a journey into an unknown land where all the roadways are new and in which we have no prior knowledge or map. It is a journey into uncertainty – a journey of mystery.

It requires faith and courage to walk through the night into the sufferings and pain of the world. 'For the fruit of the night journey will not be a soirée for a self-preoccupied spiritual élite but the realization that the world's wounds are the spaces through which God graciously enters.'[9]

> *Ray* Interestingly, international events have helped me to begin praying again – particularly the Middle East crisis, and events in Pakistan . . .

Like Job we too begin to realize we are part of something much bigger than we had previously realized. This slow dawning brings a mixture of awe, shame and excitement. John also uses another analogy, describing the journey as a mellowing and maturing process like the standing time of a good wine. In our youthful prayer and faith we, like young wine, are fresh, fizzy and liable to go off. Yet with standing time, wine and faith mature. Nothing new is added, the ingredients are all the same but something happens, the texture becomes smoother, the taste richer and the risk of 'going off' passes.[10]

John described his time imprisoned in the cistern as a time of visitation, a time of friendship with Christ as he became aware of and open to God 'increasingly sustaining, pervasive as light yet too subtle to be seized'.[11] His advice is that the journey that takes us beyond ourselves into the night is worth all the struggle and hardship, for it holds out the inestimable blessing of knowing the friendship of Christ. John wrote about it saying:

> The power of this holy night
> Dispels all evil, washes guilt away
> Restores lost innocence, brings mourners joy
> It casts out hatred, brings us peace, and humbles earthly pride.

Night truly blessed when heaven is wedded to earth
And man is reconciled with God.[12]

In this way our love for God and others is deepened until we too
can say with truth and authenticity, 'I never knew I loved so much.'
Yet it is always a personal darkness in which each of us is invited
to a different journey with God. If our journeys are always unique
then each of our nights of prayer and darkness of faith are also
unique. John says, 'God carries each person along a different road
so that you will scarcely find two people following the same route
in even half of their journey to God. Each person is unique and
God is infinitely varied.'[13] While the stories of others can be
encouraging they will never be the same as ours. Our paths are
unique; so too are our prayer lives. What is forming is a deep and
intimate relationship: a relationship between ourselves and Christ
that may have some things in common with others, but it will
never be the same for we are unique people and God interacts with
us all in personally unique ways.

I remember some years ago watching a television documentary
about nuns and the life of prayer. During an interview with the
presenter a nun in her 90s made a remarkable admission, saying,
'It is amazing that in one lifetime we can learn to touch the heart
and mind of God.' Not just that we learn to touch the heart and
mind of God but that we also learn to move and live in step with
God's heart and mind. Jean Pierre de Caussade described prayer,
saying it is that moment when 'our soul, light as a feather, fluid as
water, innocent as a child responds to every movement of grace like
a floating balloon'.[14]

Alleluia In and Beyond
Agony and Absence

It is said of God that no one can behold his face and live. I always thought this meant that no one could see his splendor and live. A friend said perhaps it meant that no one could see his sorrow and live. Or perhaps his sorrow is splendor.

(Nicholas Wolterstorff)[1]

Anne-Marie knows agony and absence. After her dad died she was asked to contribute to a book on grief and loss, something she was very willing to do. But by the time the book was published her life had been further turned upside down by another tragedy. She describes her own story:

Anne-Marie I had grown up in a Christian family. I found that the death of my dad, while painful, did not significantly challenge or alter my faith in God. Dad's heart had failed. Shit happens and suddenly it happened to me. It sucked and I hated it, but I could accept it. I'm not saying it wasn't hard. The loss was huge and it did raise questions about God and caused me to consider in a new way whether I actually believed for myself all I had grown up knowing. And I did find that God seemed painfully absent when things were most difficult. But the foundations of my faith were not hugely shaken. I stayed involved in church, started a law degree, and had the hope of life after loss.

One of the main reasons for that hope was my relationship with my boyfriend who had gently become an incredible support after the death of my dad. We had become best friends and were completely in love. He became part of the family and he was my future.

But by the time the book was finally published several years later, my world and my faith had utterly shattered, and everything I thought

I believed in profoundly challenged. Some of the things I had written about God as part of my story for the book were no longer true for me and had a hollow, meaningless ring to them. They all changed when my boyfriend killed himself. My heart broke into a million pieces that day and an all-consuming blackness exploded into my life. There are no words for the devastating impact of that death. Apart from the rest, my faith crumbled. Everything I thought I believed in came crashing down around me. This was no heart failure. Suicide is an entirely different thing. The way I understood things, a death by natural causes wasn't inconsistent with a loving God. But the kind of despair and hopelessness that drives a good, loving and vibrant person to actually kill himself, where does God figure in that?

The faith in God that I had was simply not a comfort. It seemed to me the whole thing would have been far easier to deal with if I didn't believe in God at all. C. S. Lewis said after the death of his wife, 'Talk to me about the truth of religion and I'll listen gladly. Talk to me about the duty of religion and I'll listen submissively. But don't come talking to me about the consolations of religion or I shall suspect that you don't understand.' I found God's silence deafening.[2]

As Anne-Marie was swamped by the blackness of grief and the silence of God, she encountered at a very deep and agonizing level the one universal human experience: that one thing which unites us all; the one thing we have in common with all people who walk or have ever walked this planet; that bridges all languages, ethnic groupings, political persuasions, religious ideologies, educational backgrounds and generations. What is it that we have in common with all other people, the rich and poor, academics and the illiterate, those whose lives are measured by hours and those by decades? Down through the ages philosophers and theologians from diverse backgrounds have identified one common experience – suffering. In the words of the song: 'everyone hurts sometime'. This is the common denominator which lies behind the greatest of human questions. Suffering punctures our illusions of being immortal, immune or unique while simultaneously posing the greatest threat to all beliefs, creeds and philosophies and probing to the core the unfathomable mysteries of God.

Suffering is the central theme of Annie Dillard's brilliant book *Holy the Firm*, written during a two-year stay alone in a wooden room furnished with 'one enormous window, one cat, one spider and one person'. In the book she describes the nature of suffering:

> It is less like a banana skin than a rake, the old rake in the grass, the one you step on, foot to forehead. It all comes together. In a twinkling. You have to admire it for its symmetry, accomplishing all with one right angle, the same right angle which accomplishes all philosophy. One step on the rake and it's mind under matter once again. You wake up with a piece of tree in your skull.[3]

In intense suffering the comfort of scripture, the hope of prayer and the energizing quality of faith are so often cut off from us. As Anne-Marie said:

Anne-Marie The Bible offered no comfort. All I found there was a record of broken promises. 'He will not let your foot slip'; 'A bruised reed He will not break' . . . There are hundreds of them. I could draw no comfort from these promises. No matter how much I wanted to believe it for myself, it hadn't been true for my boyfriend. He was a bruised reed that broke tragically. Time after time I discarded the Bible in anger, agony and frustration.

I couldn't pray. Pray for what? The day before my boyfriend died I knew things were hard. That night I prayed that God would stay close to him and give him the strength to get through the next day. So simple. So specific. So vital. That prayer still haunts me. I trusted God with the most important thing in my life. How could I ever pray again believing that it might make a difference? That would mean sometimes God answers prayer and therefore chose not to answer my prayer that night. The implications of that were too devastating to accept.

My faith was paralysed. What kind of God abandons somebody in that most desperate of moments? My boyfriend had loved life and loved God, and God had just let him go. I didn't know how I could ever trust God again. Anyway, what did it even mean to trust Him? Doesn't it mean that you hold on to Him as best you can and trust that when things get so bad and you're struggling to maintain your grip, that's when he keeps a tight hold of you? If you can't trust Him for that, what else matters?

I stopped going to church. At first it was just because I was in no state to go and simply couldn't face it. Then my anger and confusion with God settled in and it was an active choice not to. Over time, I felt like I just slipped away from my church unnoticed and my anger spread. I considered other churches but the longer I stayed away the harder it was to try and go again. The few times I went I just got irate and upset because I couldn't reconcile what I was hearing in church with what had happened in my life. Church and the God that I found there were completely irrelevant to what I was dealing with.

Like Dillard's rake, suffering bursts our illusions of ourselves as we drag God into our courtroom crying 'Why?' Dillard explores this universal human experience, describing the death of a moth in a candle flame and the suffering of a child burned in an aeroplane accident with complete simplicity and vividness as she moves to pose this suffering against the character of God. At one point in the book she describes faith, saying:

> Faith would be that God is self-limited utterly by his creation – a contradiction of the scope of his will; that he bound himself to time and its hazards and haps as a man would lash himself to a tree for love . . . That God is helpless, our baby to bear, self-abandoned on the doorstep of time, wondered at by cattle and oxen. Faith would be that God moved and moves once and for all and 'down', so to speak, like a diver, like a man who eternally gathers himself for a dive and eternally is diving, and eternally splitting the spread of the water, and eternally drowned.[4]

Easter, the Christian faith proclaims, is God's answer to Dillard's question. That time when the suffering of an agonizing cross, the silence and absence of death and the alleluia of resurrection collide. Easter is the record of God lashing himself as a man to a tree for love. It is the record of the alleluia heard through the agony and absence of cross and tomb. Here suffering, God and worship collide in surprising ways. The story is truncated in the Gospel of Mark. Devoid of resurrection appearances and all but one of the sayings of Jesus on the cross, Mark's Gospel ends simply with the empty tomb. There are no accounts of Thomas putting his finger into the wounds of the risen Christ, or of grave clothes being neatly stacked. There is no journey on the road to Emmaus or breakfast on the beach with the disciples. But what the Gospel of Mark does is to record the faith of one character who is given no name and about whom we have absolutely no personal information. He appears twice; each time taking up only one verse. He wasn't a follower of Jesus, he wasn't a Jew, he probably never heard Jesus teach or saw him perform a miracle, and he almost certainly never saw the risen Christ. Yet while the creeds record that Jesus was crucified under Pontius Pilate, the real work – the dirty work – was done by this man, the centurion and the soldiers under his command. While Pilate went to his lunch, a mid-day nap and a long soak in the baths it was this Roman officer who took Jesus' plight into his hands. He stood at the foot of the cross when the nails were banged into place and the cross raised. He watched as Jesus died. He is an unusual witness, one that Mark had no reason to invent. Yet it is from his lips that the Gospel records the words, 'Surely this was the Son of God'.[5]

What did the centurion see? He had surely seen crucifixions many times before. The cross had been widely used across the Empire for hundreds of years. It was something this Roman soldier had been through many times. Sometimes one or two were executed at a time, but there are also records of hundreds, even thousands, being crucified together. On this morning he walked with the three condemned men as he had walked with so many before them. Through the city streets and out of the city gate they walked towards the rubbish dump where the crosses were to be erected. The centurion was there as the soldiers stripped the robe from Jesus' back. He would have heard the cry as the scabs of congealed blood formed between flesh and cloth were ripped open. He would have supervised the nailing. He wouldn't have been surprised to see the agony on Jesus' face as the cross was dropped into the hole, or the repeated groans as he struggled to raise himself on to the nails in his feet long enough to gasp a breath, only to be overcome by the searing pain of the nails and forced to drop back down again to hang by the nails through his wrists. Up and down, agonizing breath by agonizing breath, his energy was slowly drained away. If this was someone's first experience of a crucifixion it would no doubt be a horrific experience – but this would not have been true for the centurion. He, like the soldiers squabbling over Jesus' clothes, had seen it all before.

He may have watched as the flies buzzed around Jesus' face,

over the open flesh where whip and crown had pierced, down his naked body to his legs splattered by blood, dirt and urine. He'd seen it all before. And yet something captured his attention and held this career soldier's gaze. Was it Jesus' acceptance of his suffering and death? The way he refused to answer Pilate's questions? In Mark's account Jesus only speaks once at Pilate's trial, responding to Pilate's question: 'Are you the king of the Jews?' with the words 'Yes, it is as you say.' There is no fighting, no struggling, no bargaining or begging. The centurion observes this acceptance of death and suffering. This willingness to go all the way, as the writer of the letter to the Hebrews wrote: 'Although he was a son, he learned obedience from what he suffered.'[6]

He listened to the one cry from the cross recorded by Mark: 'My God, my God, why have you forsaken me?' The limit of words possible from one breath as nailed feet punctuated his prayer. This prayer was at once a cry of Christ's reality, abandonment and alienation wedded to the cry of relationship and faith: 'My God, my God.'

While listening to his prayer as death approached, a fuller reality dawned on the centurion. Here was suffering: suffering at a depth and intensity he had never seen before. The cup willingly taken from the hand of this man's God. 'Surely this was the Son of God,' he said.

The centurion was not convinced by Jesus' teaching or miracles, he was not swayed by the empty tomb or resurrection appearances; what captivated his heart and implanted faith was Christ's suffering. He didn't need more evidence of Christ's power; his identification with humanity was what mattered. For in his suffering the authenticity of Christ was shown. This centurion, the very best judge we could have at such a moment, was convinced: 'This was the Son of God.'

In the midst of our world of suffering and pain this is the conviction we need as well. As Dietrich Bonhoeffer, imprisoned in a Nazi cell awaiting torture and death, wrote repeatedly: 'Only a suffering God will do.'[7] In our own sufferings this mantra of Bonhoeffer carries increased weight. Only a God who enters and experiences our suffering will do. It is a plea picked up by Edward Shillito writing from the trenches of World War I:

If we have never sought, we seek Thee now;
Thine eyes burn through the dark, our only stars;
We must have sight of thorn-marks on Thy brow,
We must have Thee, O Jesus of the scars.

The other gods were strong, but Thou wast weak;
They rode, but Thou didst stumble to a throne;
But to our wounds only God's wounds can speak,
And not a god has wounds, but Thou alone.[8]

The scriptures say you can't see the glory of God and live, maybe the suffering of God is his glory and we could not observe this suffering of God and survive.[9] If so, this centurion saw enough to know this could only be God. It is what Annie Dillard longs for in *Holy the Firm*; God identifying with. Not just identifying with; but God shattered and dying. God suffering and pained as we are. God dying, scarred and dirty in every sense but also fully God in every sense. The two in one. Suffering and glory wedded. The universal human reality locked into the reality of God. Holy God yet firm and real, encompassed in suffering and death. This is what the centurion saw. Is this why he drew close and looked carefully, seeing not just another madman, criminal or political activist dying on a cross like so many others he had seen before, but Jesus Christ?

Here, in the midst of Good Friday's suffering and pain, we see two statements of worship: one from the mouth of Christ and one from the centurion – neither one denying or minimizing the enormity of the suffering and alienation of the moment but in both heartfelt and authentic worship. In one obedience even to a cross with the words 'My God, my God'. Words full of personal connection and conviction. God exists for Christ even in this moment when his face is hidden and God has abandoned him. Christ's abandonment and God's absence have not stolen from him the faith that God is. And this God is his God. This is worship in the midst of the storm – 'My God, my God.' Like the prayers of Job reduced to a profound simplicity. And then the statement of the centurion, again simple conviction without any gloss: 'Surely this was the Son of God.' Here we see the worship of the dark night. The praise of the desert. Faithful suffering when God hides his face. Gone is the exuberance of songs and dancing: the words are direct and simple, yet they carry every ounce of who we are. Surely this is authentic worship when the lights go out. This is a very hard place. Perhaps it would seem easier if we really were abandoned rather than sensing God is there and we are still abandoned. It would be easier, we cry, if God didn't exist at all; if I didn't even believe in God. Not surprisingly, some people move in this direction.

Anne-Marie says of her own experience:

> *Anne-Marie* Even though most of the time I felt like I was crying out into a void I didn't really ever stop believing in God. Actually, there were probably times when I did, there was just so much emptiness. But mostly it was more that I felt like I didn't understand the true nature of God and how he interacts with the world. I couldn't accept there are things we will never understand and we just have to accept them and trust God. That would have been to deny the enormous impact of what had happened, to pretend it somehow didn't matter because after all God's got it all under control and he must have his reasons. No way was I settling for that. I needed to understand more than I did before trust was going to become an option again.

The women at the cross must have carried this same mix of emptiness and doubt as they watched Jesus slowly dying in front of them. As darkness comes they and Joseph of Arimathea in their silent worship take the body from the centurion carefully wrapping it in clean linen, and place it in the tomb. So their silent worship, quietly active, generously giving and compassionately caring, takes over. Now the long, silent waiting of Easter Saturday begins. Easter Saturday is such a flat day. Gone is all the action of Good Friday, the trial and cross, while Easter Sunday with the triumphant cries of the women, the running of the disciples and the first of the resurrection appearances has not yet arrived. There is just the blackness of Easter Saturday when we remember Jesus' body lying in the blackness of a borrowed tomb. In this blackness, when the depth of the disciples and the women's true feelings dominate, the Gospels remain silent. On this black day when God's absence is palpable, silence pervades.

So too in our own personal dark nights of faith, when our only sense of God is his absence, our honest worship is silence: a silence that waits. When the songs and exuberance of past worship utterly repulse us a much quieter, slower and more reflective approach can more authentically shape our worship. This is the worship of the women who wait in silence for the dawn to come. This is the truth that Handel conveys as he juxtaposes next to the 'Hallelujah' chorus the prayer of Job from the midst of his own blackness: 'I know that my redeemer liveth, and that he shall stand at the latter day upon the earth: And though worms destroy this body, yet in my flesh shall I see God.'[10] Handel does not include Job's next sentence when he says, 'Yes, I will see him for myself, and I long for that moment.'[11] Here again the quiet faith full waiting. This worship of darkness; the silent waiting on the desert path. The waiting that cannot hurry the dawn and may not even see it, as Job says, on this side of the grave. Yet is willing to wait in silence, as a mother waits out the night with a sick child.

For Moses, and later the people of God in the desert, this is when they meet God in a new way. Through burning bush and mountaintop God reveals himself to them. As Job in the darkness of his suffering is presented with a God who is much bigger and much more intimately involved in everything than he was previously willing to imagine, so too long after the women would have hoped, the dawn does come. As the deep blackness before the dawn is punctuated by the first glimpses of light, they can now stop their waiting and go to the tomb in time to see the Son risen. There is their new perspective, the chrysalis of their waiting cracking, the invitation to enter a new realm.

So the Easter remembrance ends with the 'Hallelujah' of Sunday's worship: the cry of new life beyond death; the worship of the second naïveté of faith that Paul Ricoeur spoke of. That worship that knots the dual realities of life in all its suffering, darkness and pain with the reality of God is intimately connected to all realities, but now aware of the new possibilities of God: the butterfly invited to fly from the place of waiting; Moses invited to go back to Egypt and lead his people out of slavery; Job invited to rebuild his family and his farm; the invitation given to the prodigal son in the father's embrace. It is not the forgetting of the past or the denying of all that was learnt and felt during the night, but it is the transcending of these realities into the greater realities of God. And so the 'Hallelujah' which means 'Praise Yahweh' rings out; that which was dead is alive.

Anne-Marie In the midst of all the useless platitudes I was offered when my boyfriend died, as people tried to make sense of it and tried to defend God, the most comforting and empowering thing anyone said to me went something like: 'Scream at God, cry out to Him and let Him know you're angry and disappointed . . . but remember the man hanging on the cross.'

In the Easter story's agony, absence and alleluia we see a maturity of faith-full worship. At each point, agony, absence and alleluia, there is the possibility of genuine worship. Worship that carries the sense of agony in screams of pain, the worship of stillness and waiting as darkness and death envelop, and at the right time the early morning alleluia as new life and faith emerge. In too much modern worship there is only room for a shallow alleluia, leaving our faith and worship severely impoverished.

8

Growth and Grace
In and Beyond Failure

◄○►

At least there is hope for a tree:
   If it is cut down, it will sprout again,
   and its new shoots will not fail.
Its roots may grow old in the ground
   and its stump die in the soil,
yet at the scent of water it will bud
   and put forth shoots.[1]

Having considered two metaphors for the difficult terrain of faith crises and some of the common themes and issues faced in the desert places and dark times, it is time to consider two more specific themes which loom very largely for many people, those of failure and suspicion. We will begin with failure. Failure is very difficult to face in both ourselves and others; perhaps therefore it is a good theme with which to begin.

Failure is not an 'in' word. Wherever it is mentioned in business, family life, the media or in Christian circles, failure is often seen as the unforgivable. At all costs, failure is to be hidden. Our culture is failure averse. Yet the stories of scripture, unlike modern culture, are quite the opposite. They are full of failure. A cursory look reminds us that Adam and Eve failed to keep the one thing God asked of them. Cain murdered his brother. Noah got drunk, acted improperly and then cursed his sons. Noah's sons built the tower of Babel. Abraham lied to the Egyptians and called his wife his sister, causing her to be taken into Pharaoh's harem. Lot was involved in incest. Esau and Jacob quarrelled over their rights as sons. Joseph's brothers sold him into slavery. The book of Genesis is full of immorality, deceit and self-promotion. After the enslavement in Egypt, Moses killed, the people complained and made

87

idols to foreign gods and initially refused to cross into the Promised Land. The people's first King (Saul) was a disaster. He was jealous and tried to kill David on a number of occasions and was completely self-absorbed. David, the next in line for the throne, although he had many wives and concubines, seduced another man's wife and then tried to cover up his failure by killing her husband. Solomon built a wonderful temple but fell victim to his own success and failed God. The tribes of Israel failed to get along and split the kingdom in two. Of the list of kings of the two kingdoms the vast majority followed pagan gods and treated their own people poorly. Yet if we go to a passage like Hebrews 11, which lists the heroes and heroines of the faith, we find many of the same people who had failed God repeatedly. Adulterers, murderers, prostitutes, liars and drunkards – they are all there, these heroes and heroines of the faith. The very people who would receive a cool welcome at church today.

The New Testament is little better. Judas betrayed Jesus to the authorities. Peter denied Jesus to the people gathered around the fire. All the disciples ran and hid as Jesus was tried and executed. Paul began by persecuting the Church. Then he and Barnabas squabbled and had to separate. He had to point out the failures of Peter and the other followers who were afraid of public opinion, and yet Paul, recognizing his own weakness and failure, introduced himself as the least of all the apostles;[2] one not even worthy to be called an apostle. When we look at the early Church we find failure as a common theme. Read through the letters to the Corinthians and you will see everything imaginable including immorality 'so terrible that not even the heathen would be guilty of it'.[3]

Yet the New Testament, like the Old, commends these people as people who followed after God and were friends of God[4] and on occasion as people who had the same heart as God.[5] Equally the Bible narrative does not hide their failure and their weakness; in fact, after reading through the lives of the key characters of the Bible we could be excused for thinking that failure is a necessary qualification for a part in God's unfolding story.

In New Zealand and Australia, ANZAC Day is remembered with a growing national pride. Ironically ANZAC day commemorates a military failure. On this annual holiday increasing numbers of people go to dawn parades and church services in order to remember the day. There are also growing numbers of young people touring to Europe to be on the beaches of Gallipoli in order to remember this particular anniversary. Increasingly it is a day which marks an important part of Kiwi and Australian identity. It serves today as a point of strength, pride and a marker of national identity. This is an identity born from failure. The Christian faith is very similar. The key event is the cross. The instrument by which the King of Glory was brutally slaughtered. A place of tremendous failure and horror and yet now a stable point of identity for hundreds of millions and a symbol of peace. Can it be the same for us individually? Can the site of our personal failure become a place of identity and pride? We talk of God forgiving us and taking away our failure, yet I wonder how often this is a conceptual and distant thought: something that we know about in theory but not so much in the reality of our lives. Dietrich Bonhoeffer, the German theologian and activist, came to a point like this in his own faith when imprisoned by the Nazis, and facing his own imminent execution he said he moved from 'phraseology to reality'.[6] His most famous biographer and friend Eberhard Bethge said, 'The theologian became a Christian.'[7] This marked a key point in his life where what he knew intellectually and conceptually became more than just words; it became personal and real in a much deeper way.

We are considering what it means to be called again. To be called again is to be invited into a new depth and proximity of relationship with God. This new call, the second call, can come in and beyond failure. Rarely is this call heard until we have fallen flat on our faces and had our noses rubbed into our weakness and failure. From this perspective failure is not an impediment to a deepening of faith but most often a necessary pathway. In our failures lies the hope of new beginnings.

There are, of course, different types of failure: the failure to succeed in which an expected goal is not reached; personal failure in which we let ourselves and others down by not doing what we could do or doing what we 'shouldn't' have done; and then there is the failure of 'falling' – that moral failure that undermines our position as leaders, as followers of Christ, perhaps even as moral people. When we fall in such ways this type of failure can be worsened if we have hurt not only ourselves but also others through our abuse of power, position or knowledge in a way that damages others.

A close friend's experience in a Third World mission context provides an example of the first type of failure – failure in an expected goal. He, his wife and family had moved from successful work in New Zealand to a Third World pioneer mission context. They put everything they had into the work, lived in the kind of poverty and difficulty the people they were trying to serve also lived within, and suffered huge personal and family adjustments and hardships. In the end much of their hard work and dreams came to nothing. As he himself wrote: 'Months of hard work was now rendered suspect. Some of us felt like failures. We had believed, prayed and even fasted over the years. We had poured our lives into the work. And yet despite all of this, the work was now crumbling around us.' Responses from supporters at home were less than helpful as he wrote home explaining what had happened and the mistakes they now saw they had made. Speaking more personally he went on to write:

> Over the coming months I sagged into a crisis of faith. We had stopped many of our programs, our churches dwindled in numbers, missionaries were leaving, and some of our prized converts were falling away. It was all coming apart.
>
> It seemed that being a believer in Christ made no difference at all. Faith, prayer, clean living, and hard work counted for little. In the face of poverty all of these were rendered ineffective and powerless. I was losing that certainty about God, Jesus Christ and the Holy Spirit. Right and wrong, good and bad began to blur. I began to doubt whether there was a place any more for the Christian virtues, godly disciplines and spirituality.
>
> I had read of how social workers, missionaries, pastors and priests who had immersed themselves among the poor, had ended up disillusioned cripples clutching a bottle, hoping to escape the memories of their failures. I now understand how this could happen. I began to drink. Not only that, but one night I came very close to doing something very stupid with an attractive neighbour of ours. I was not coping too well. The losses of the past four years were beginning to catch up on me. The loss of New Zealand, the loss of comfort, security and health; the loss of Joseph [their newborn baby who died], and the loss of the loan scheme.[8]

Many people wouldn't call this failure, quoting verses like 'And we know that in all things God works for the good of those who love him'[9] but it certainly felt that way to Eldon.

A less understandable failure is the personal moral failure of Christians, especially Christian leaders, who 'fall': the kind of failure that occurs when personal addictions take control and sexual, financial or power abuse follows. Such failure is much harder to deal with. Not only are dreams and goals not reached but personal expectations and the expectations of others have been consciously violated. Such wounds are very hard to treat. What most often happens is that we move into a process of denial, hiding and damage control. This is clearly not the model presented in scripture where failure and forgiveness, weakness and God's strength are intimately related and neither is hidden or minimized in the text. Sadly, this is often not the case in the Church as many modern Christians do not seem to have the same attitudes towards failure as the writers of the biblical narratives. Today failure is invariably hidden. Look at the way the Catholic Church (and it is certainly not restricted to Catholic churches) in many countries of the world hides systemic historical abuse. It is not dealt with openly. The end result is that individual Christians are disqualified, the Church and Christian faith are publicly lampooned and God's ongoing work in people's lives is thwarted. Finally, when things come to the surface that have been hidden, they are often much worse than they could have been if they were dealt with earlier. Sadly, at this point the person is often made into something similar to an Old Testament scapegoat as Christians and often wider society lump on them not simply their own failure but the communities' anger, fear, and personal sense of guilt.

When a church pursues a desire for perfection in people and an unwillingness to accept failure in others, and therefore in themselves, a very warped expression of Christian faith results. If a church doesn't experience and offer grace and forgiveness or tries to hide its feet of clay and put on masks, all you are left with is a sham. It is not biblical and it is not helpful. It has far more in common with the Pharisees of Jesus' time: those self-professed 'good and holy people' Jesus called a sham. Why do we suspect God looks in any different way today? They were the ones Jesus spent as little time with as possible, preferring to be with people who knew about failure, their own failure – tax collectors, sinners, the morally broken and societally despised. The sort of people who had no problem saying, 'I'm a failure and I need help.'

The stark reality is that each of us at some point in the journey will fail. I don't mean a little hiccup that everyone could understand and which could be talked about politely over scones in a home-group discussion. I don't mean the failures we admit to as modern Christians – that we aren't reading our Bibles as often as we would like, or some equally inane slip-up. I mean fail in a way we desperately want to hide. Fail in a way that we are embarrassed. When this happens, we too face the choice: either to try and hide and pretend nothing happened by putting on masks to cover our reality; simply to give up on trying to live Christian lives and walk away; or the initially very difficult and courageous option to face up to what we have done. In the end these are the only options. The biblical option is clear. The Bible doesn't try to sanitize or sweep under the carpet people's failures, no matter how embarrassing they might have been. It seems the Bible deals with failure in such an upfront and honest way for two reasons. First, it reminds us that the biblical characters, like us, are very ordinary people. People that we, because of their failures and weaknesses, can identify with. Second, because, the agenda of the Bible is to show how God is at work and not to make individuals within it look great.

If there is some truth in these points, what does it say about our approach to failure? What does it say about our approach to others who have failed? Do we have a theology of failure?

> The central claim of Christianity is that we are accepted in our sinfulness, forgiven and understood as we are, with all our moral confusions, both of intellect and will, understood when we do not do what is right . . . God knew, understands, forgives and offers us the divine love, the divine mercy . . . that's why it is good news and not good advice.[10]

If we look at a passage at the end of John's Gospel[11] we are reminded of the risen Christ meeting with the disciples on the beach in the early hours of the morning. Prior to Jesus' crucifixion Peter had promised never to leave Jesus and even to 'lay down' his life for Jesus.[12] Only a few hours later Peter, caught up in his own confusion and powerlessness, does the very thing he thought he would never do; in fact the very thing he thought he could never do. Up to this point Peter was always confident, self-assured and independent. While he willingly left his boats and nets to follow Jesus he remains very much in control of what he says and does. In Peter there is a natural vitality, strong-headedness and self-determination. Though Jesus said things directly to Peter, including saying he would disown him[13] and that he didn't know what Jesus was doing[14] Peter remained self-assured and self-reliant. When he does disown Jesus[15] his whole sense of self and his 'self-truth' collapses. Who Peter thought he was and what he thought he could commit to and control was shown to be beyond him. The shadows of fear and confusion had overwhelmed him as he ended up doing the very thing he felt he would never do.

Notice that when Jesus came to call Peter this second time it was again early in the morning after they had shared a meal of fish together by the Sea of Galilee. It is almost like a repetition of the first time Peter had encountered Jesus. It is by the same sea,[16] again after the disciples had been fishing, in a place and context that Peter knew well and was proficient in. It was here that this second decisive encounter between Christ and Peter was to take place. When they came ashore, Peter, dripping wet and no doubt cold in the cool morning air, saw that Jesus had a fire burning. It had been burning for some time and the wood had burned down to the red-hot coals that gave a constant heat for cooking. Jesus already had fish cooking but asked that they bring some of the enormous catch they had just caught[17] to add to the breakfast. Jesus' words to the disciples are so practical, so human, so welcoming: 'Come and have breakfast.'[18] As they gathered round the fire Jesus infused the moment with even greater poignancy as he took bread, broke it and gave it to them. Then he took the fish and did the same. John goes on to record that after they had finished eating, Jesus spoke personally with Simon Peter.

Jesus said to Simon Peter, 'Simon son of John, do you love me more than these others do?' Jesus addressed Peter as Simon the son of John. In so doing he took him back to their first meeting[19] and addressed him personally and intimately. Jesus asked, 'Do you love me more than these?' This could be taken to mean 'more than these boats and fishing gear', 'more than you love these other disciples', or 'more than these other disciples love me'. The Good News Bible translates the verse as 'Do you love me more than these others do?', which is the way most commentators understand the sentence; but if they are right it makes a curious statement from Jesus' lips. Jesus is not normally into comparisons of one person's love or commitment against another's. Why would he be doing this now? Here we have a personal encounter between Simon and Jesus. Simon had always been so bold about his devotion and loyalty to Jesus, saying, 'These others will leave you but I never will. I will always be there for you. I'll die with you.' This is part of Peter's own truth. His loyalty and commitment to Jesus is something which he held and prized. It is something that Jesus was now pointing to because Peter's deepest truth and ambition was something that in his own strength Peter couldn't keep. Jesus, in typical fashion, went straight to the heart of the issue. He was acknowledging how much Peter's denial of him had deeply grieved and hurt Peter. Luke's Gospel records Peter's reaction when he realized what he had done: 'He went outside and wept bitterly.'[20] Where Peter thought he was strong, he was in fact weak. This is not a tearing down of Peter's 'gift' but an acknowledgement that his greatest gift also has a shadow side – a weakness and a vulnerability to failure. This is true for all of us. And it is only as we encounter, own and acknowledge this reality that we can come to the place of grace and growth beyond failure.

The failing of Peter and many other biblical characters is not just a peripheral issue but failure that strikes at the very heart of their place of strength and conviction. Failure at the very point where they felt they were able to achieve. Failure in the most important of areas for them. Perhaps it is only as we encounter, own, acknowledge and grieve this personal failure that we know the desert of failure and the grace and growth that God offers through it.

Our failure, like a glacier, carves a deep, raw hole in the landscape of our lives and our soul, leaving a gaping wound which is embarrassingly seen by others. Like the aftermath of failure, a glacier cuts deep, slowly, grindingly. With time the glacial hole can become the site of a beautiful lake or running river as the open wound left by the glacial path is filled by the fresh rainwaters that invariably come. Initially the rainwater simply makes muddy puddles but, given time, the mud settles and clear waters are left. New Zealand has many such lakes, deep and blue; stunningly beautiful. It is slow though – glaciers move slowly, carving deeply.

The deeper the failure, the deeper our wound and potentially the deeper the final pool of God's grace.

That's what grace and growth beyond failure means for each one of us. Each one of us has a personal truth, a personal gift and strength that we long to use. It may be that we are good and morally upright, it may be that we are loyal, that we care and act lovingly, it may be that we see and can discern what is going on, it may be that we bring laughter and happiness into the lives of others. It may be any number of things. These things are deeply ingrained and part of who we are and therefore part of what we want to give God. And sooner or later we may fail in this most important of areas and be faced, as Peter was, with that second calling of Christ – the call in and beyond failure.

What is the grace that God offers? 'Grace is not passive acceptance or unconditional disregard. Nor is it God's divine amnesty, as if he was a nice tolerant deity and accepts us regardless of what we do . . . Grace is God's reconciliation and recreation of humankind in Jesus Christ.'[21] Such graceful forgiveness does not mean forgetting or denial, it does not mean a condoning of what was done. It does not mean excusing what was done. Neither does it mean condemning or seeking compensation. What it means is 'the forgoing of resentment or revenge when the wrongdoer's actions deserve it and giving the gifts of mercy, generosity and love when the wrongdoer does not deserve them'.[22] Jesus confronts Peter with a question that is repeated three times: 'Simon son of John, do you truly love me more than these?' The first time the question is asked, Peter replied, saying 'You know that I love you.' His answer is correct because he obviously does love Christ but no longer does he make a claim to loving him in a way that is superior or greater to the other disciples. He knows now that he cannot offer that. The second time Jesus asks the question he does not include the comparison with the other disciples; rather he simply asks, 'Simon son of John, do you truly love me?' Notice again the very personal naming of Simon not as Peter the rock but using his own given name and identifying him with his Father. This is a very intimate and personal calling. Lacking the comparative question, Simon is able to say, 'Yes, Lord, you know that I love you.' His answer acknowledges the way Christ can see deeply into him and already knows the answer. The third and final time Jesus asks the question he chooses exactly the same words. It is the same question. We are told that this asking of the same question for the third time hurt Peter. Why? Because Jesus was not satisfied with the answer; he wanted something more. Peter gives it to him, saying what he had never said before: 'Lord, you know all things . . .'[23]

In Peter's answer a new humility is shown and a new trust is born. He is saying 'Lord, I think, I believe, maybe even I hope that I love you, but you know more than I do. I used to think I knew myself and was confident in myself. Now I realize you know me better than I know myself and that there are contradictions and shadows within me far more powerful than I ever realized.' Hearing this, Jesus tells Peter that to follow means looking after those who are also committed to Christ and in time it will mean giving away his fierce independence even to the point that others will dress him and lead him where he does not want to go. For Peter to follow Christ will mean being involved in the care and support of Christ's people. To follow will mean giving up his independence even to the most basic of levels.

Peter then looks at John and asks about his friend. What will it cost John to follow Jesus? Why is Jesus only focusing the full effect of accepting the call to follow on Peter? To this Jesus replies, saying, 'What is that to you? You must follow me.'[24]

The example of Peter is crucial at the point of significant and deep personal failure, because here we face the bankruptcy of our own strength, our own integrity and perhaps our own morality. We are broken, we are less than what we purported to be and less than what we ourselves believed we were. The way ahead is a real desert or dark night. The way back to where we were and who we were is cut off. We cannot now simply go back. We too must follow the followers of scripture by naming our failure – naming it specifically, totally and honestly and not trying to pretend it is anything but failure. As well as fully and completely naming the failure, the emotional pain of anger, hurt, hatred and distress must be faced. We must grieve for our own failure and weaknesses. The hurt we have caused ourselves takes some time to heal. During this time the pain we may have caused others and God needs to be felt. Only then can we move into God's deeper grace, as Peter does here: grace based on reconciliation of relationship and love. This reconciliation can only follow in the wake of a broken and damaged relationship. We cannot ask God to repair what we will not acknowledge and own as being broken. Finally, in God's grace and providence we may find ourselves making leaps of growth that we would not have been able to make previously. It often takes time though; glacial movement is slow. This grace is offered to Peter as Jesus also gives him a task to do. Jesus explains the hardships ahead, and finally says 'Follow me.'

This incident is crucial for Peter. Later he writes, 'As the scripture says, 'You have found out for yourselves how kind the Lord is.'[25] Paul, the religious mass murderer, knew this too, claiming God says, 'My kindness is all you need. My power is strongest when you are weak.'[26] And later, owning the truth himself, saying: 'For when I am weak then I am strong.'[27] To know and know deeply what Peter and Paul claim here is not based on a general sense of failure and personal weakness. This is not a conceptual or theological reality but something which is far more personalized and realized. Peter and Paul are talking about themselves and their own lives. It is only when we travel a similar journey of personal failure into the deserts of shame, guilt and humiliation that we can taste the depths of grace and growth offered to us in Christ's new calling. The call comes not in spite of, but specifically, because of the specific way we have failed. Oh, to taste such grace and know when I am weak then I am strong. When we too can say Jesus forgave me . . . and in my weakness and 'gutted-ness' he gave me new hope and strength. Yet we so often hide our failures and let them grow and erode us inwardly. In so doing we miss the call beyond the desert of failure: the call to grace and growth.

St John of the Cross describes this process, using the image of a piece of wood placed in an open fire to illustrate the transforming process that God is working in and through our failure. The log of wood is ourselves, the fire the purifying work of God. The end result will be complete unity of fire and log, but to get to there the log is transformed. St John writes that the fire

> . . . when applied to wood, first dehumidifies it, dispelling all moisture and making it give off any water it contains; then it gradually turns the wood black, making it dark and ugly, and even causes it to emit a bad odour . . . The fire brings to light and expels all those ugly and dark accidents which are contrary to fire.[28]

Father Thomas Green in his comments about this passage points out that the experience of the log, should it have one, must be both painful and alarming as the fire dries it out, turns it black and ugly, revealing all the cracks and flaws, and forces the maggots and insects to the surface. Green says, 'If the log could think, it would say to itself: "This is a disaster! Far from becoming beautiful, I am much uglier than before. I have made a terrible mistake in submitting to the fire."'[29] Yet all that has happened is that which was hidden has been revealed. The truth is forced to the surface and, as Jesus said, 'The truth will set you free.' St John continues:

> Finally, by heating and enkindling the fire transforms the wood into itself and makes it as beautiful as it is itself. Once transformed, the wood no longer has any activity or passivity of its own . . . For it possesses the properties and performs the actions of the fire.[30]

Through our failure our own truth can be brought to the surface. John says, 'through the paradox of the flame that burns in pain to the flame that burns in love; O delicious wound – the flame that liberates and brings a deep inner peace and joy.'[31] When denial, hiding and false limiting of our own failure are overcome the transformation of self through grace is possible. For, as James claimed, when we confess our sin to each other and pray for each other we may be healed.[32]

9

Trust In and Beyond Suspicion

———◁◦▷———

Russell I wanted to be legitimated in my experience, I wanted people to understand; and my experience is that people in church leadership will not understand. They don't have the capacity to understand. Some probably do, but that is how I react instinctively. I don't trust them. I'm not willing to trust. I entrusted myself for so many years. I know the sort of passion and commitment I put into it. I generally find that people like that have an agenda; they can't love as human beings. Obviously there are exceptions to this, but that is my experience. And maybe they could but I'm not willing to give them a chance. It really comes down to the fact that I don't think people know how to love . . . able to love in a way that they can include others without being threatened. They can't embrace others' realities. That's something I haven't felt. People haven't embraced my whole reality.

Russell's comments indicate the degree of hurt, broken trust, alienation and anger expressed by people whose trust in the Church has been violated. When he says, 'I don't trust them. I'm not willing to trust . . . I'm not willing to give them a chance' we can feel something of the depth of pain and continued hurt the broken trust by Christian leaders has left him with. It is neither an uncommon nor an outrageous response to the way he was treated. Sadly Russell is not alone. In formal research and informal conversations I have heard horrific stories of broken trust and spiritual abuse. Although cushioned by the conventions of research and my own relatively thick hide, the pain of these stories has often haunted me long into the night. Jamie's experience illustrates the impact of broken trust further.

Jamie I've got a relative who was held up in the church as a paragon of virtue . . . He was someone who accepted the hardships of Christian life, self-sacrifice, moral behaviour, steadfast in the face of societal rejection, the whole bit, strong, resolute. So here was this person who I looked up to. It came out that he had been sexually molesting his kids. But when I found this out, you know, I just thought, this is all crap, and I thought, argh, let me out of here, I'm sick of this.

A common theme among church leaders I have spoken with is the disillusionment and broken trust felt by people when key church leaders fail in some way. A disillusionment that many church leaders credit as the reason people give up on church or the Christian faith, perhaps both. As one pastor said about people's reasons for leaving church: 'It is usually out of deep disappointment and disillusionment with leadership, either leadership decisions or poor counselling.' An aspect of leadership disillusionment that is mentioned regularly by pastors and ministers was the number of situations where church leaders had 'fallen' and subsequently disillusioned large numbers of people. Often this involves situations where pastors were found to be involved in adulterous relationships and/or financial impropriety. In these cases there appeared to be a general understanding that where significant leaders 'fell' there was a high degree of disillusionment and people subsequently left the church. I have also interviewed many leavers who had been involved in churches where the senior pastor had 'fallen' in some spectacular fashion and yet no one identified this as a major factor in their decision to leave. While such events undoubtedly caused disillusionment with that leader and often leaders in general, and motivated some to move churches, no one identified this as the principal or sole reason for their leaving altogether. On the contrary, many discussed the disappointment of being deceived by a leader as a situation through which their faith in God had strengthened and matured as they learned to be less dependent on church leaders. Interestingly, a more important factor in their decision to stay or leave the church was based on how the leadership elected to handle the difficulty. Where it was hidden, swept under the carpet and not openly dealt with, people lost a greater degree of confidence in the leadership.

In the last chapter we considered being called, as Peter was, in and beyond personal failure. The only way through, it was suggested, was by openly acknowledging the failure and seeking to own responsibly its impact on others. It is something churches must also consider. There is another side to this as well. Because facing our own personal failure and learning to forgive ourselves is connected to a growing compassion and understanding of the failures of others, being able to trust ourselves again and moving beyond a pervading personal suspicion of our own weaknesses and inadequacies provides a model for doing the same with others. The Lord's Prayer, for example, makes this connection by linking our forgiveness with our forgiveness of others, remembering that to forgive does not mean a removal of the pain and hurt we may carry. The wounds of others can be deep, and we may hurt for a very long time. The fact that we continue to feel this hurt and pain does not mean we are unable to forgive or have failed to forgive. Forgiveness does not equal forgetting.

Helmut Thielicke, a German pastor who endured the darkest days of the Nazi Third Reich, is quoted as saying: 'One should never mention the words "Forgive and forget" in the same breath. No, we will remember, but in forgiving we no longer use the memory against others. Forgiveness is not pretending the event never occurred, or that it does not matter. It did matter, and there is no use pretending otherwise. The offence is real, but when we forgive, the offence no longer controls our behaviour. It is not acting as if things are just the same as they were before the offence . . . they will never be the same.'

By the grace of God they can be a thousand times better, but they can never be the same. Such forgiveness sets in place a stepping stone to a trust beyond suspicion. But it is not just the church or individual Christian leaders that break trust. For some people the real issue is directly with God. Remember Anne-Marie's sense that God had let her down when she had prayed for her boyfriend, or consider William and Jennifer's sense of broken trust as they prayed for Jennifer's brother with no reply:

Anne-Marie I couldn't pray. Pray for what? The day before my boyfriend died I knew things were hard. That night I prayed that God would stay close to him and give him the strength to get through the next day. So simple. So specific. So vital. That prayer still haunts me. I trusted God with the most important thing in my life.

101

How could I ever pray again believing that it might make a difference? That would mean sometimes God answers prayer and therefore chose not to answer my prayer that night. The implications of that were too devastating to accept.

William There were a few instances that we really believed God for, that didn't work out the way we thought. This was a real step of faith and it just didn't happen. Some people would say that it just means that God was saying the answer was no. But I was really convinced it was going to happen. We believed we were doing everything we should, but nothing happened. There were a couple of those. Jennifer's brother, we spent a lot of time praying with him and talking and really, we thought we were doing the right thing. Praying that the marriage would come back together again. And it didn't. And it affected our faith in God and him working.

These are not 'Give-me-a-car-park-space prayers', but deep, heartfelt prayers from trusting people that, it would seem, have been returned with no answer. How do people rebuild a sense of trust when the trust they had has been so badly crushed?

The story of Cleopas and his friend walking down the road to Emmaus[1] may help us here. These two friends who are described as followers of Jesus are going back to their village, back home, after Jesus' trial and crucifixion. These two had hoped that Jesus was the one who was going to set Israel free. They had heard him speak, seen him interacting with people, interacted with him themselves, and knew enough about him to have put their trust in him and call themselves his followers. They had invested their hopes and dreams for the future in Jesus who they believed would redeem Israel. But then it all fell apart; in a very short space of time Jesus was crucified and what had seemed all very stable and secure in their lives was suddenly turned upside down. The expectations they had put their trust in were totally undermined and as far as they could see had now completely fallen apart. As they are walking back to Emmaus they were down in the dumps, despondent and disillusioned. No doubt they were eyewitnesses to the last days of Jesus' life and were now convinced that he was dead. Down in the dumps too were their hopes and trust. The let-down must have been enormous.

As they were walking they were discussing the recent shattering events, trying to come to grips with it all. They were confused and had a keen sense that their trust had been betrayed as they carried the full weight of all these unfulfilled expectations.

Cleopas and his friend trusted and believed that Jesus would redeem Israel but they had built certain ideas about how that would happen. In their minds was probably something more triumphant and obvious – it certainly didn't include the fact that Jesus would be mocked, remain silent at trial and be crucified. They were grappling with this disillusionment as Jesus, who they didn't recognize, drew alongside and walked with them. Jesus listened to what they were talking about, enabling them to express their grief and their dashed hopes and disappointment. 'But we had hoped that he would be the one who was going to set Israel free. Besides all that, this is now the third day since it happened.'[2] Together with Jesus they had quite a long time to process all this as the journey was a walk of seven miles.

As they talked, Jesus challenged their illusions saying, 'How foolish you are, how slow you are to believe everything the prophets said! Was it not necessary for the Messiah to suffer these things and then to enter his glory?'[3] and he went on more gently to explain to them what was said in the scriptures concerning himself. They didn't know the background to this man, they hadn't grasped the wider picture and so didn't understand much of what he was saying.

By the time they got to their village they had sensed enough about their travelling companion to risk inviting him to stay with them. Although confused, they had heard enough to want to carry on the conversation. But it wasn't until the stranger did a very familiar thing – breaking bread – that they recognized who he was. And as soon they realized, he left them. He had come alongside just long enough to help them rethink the illusion and rekindle the flame inside them. He stayed with them just long enough for them to be called to trust again, this time with a deeper and more inner knowing. As they recalled their encounter they said, 'Were not our hearts burning within us while he talked with us on the road and opened the Scriptures to us?'[4] This time it was not a naïve trust but one based on a deeper reality in the knowledge of who Jesus was and of his purposes. It was a determined action, a renewed commitment: 'They got up immediately and went back to Jerusalem to join the group of followers.'[5]

At various points on the journey of faith we too discover that God is not where we thought God would be and even, perhaps, who we thought God was. We realize we haven't got God figured at all. With the destruction of our image of God we come to sense that maybe the image we had wasn't a very good one after all. We had placed God in a box. Maybe the church or Christian group we had been a part of sold us this boxed image of God. Maybe it was an image of our own making. Wherever our image of God came from, it is broken, now irredeemably broken, and in good faith we can never go back to it. We either come to see God in a new light or we cease to search after God at all.

The journey of faith often involves a complete breakdown in our understanding of God and Christian faith followed by a period of chaos and uncertainty and then a slow rebuilding of understanding that is much broader and deeper than what we had held to previously. This is normal. Knowing it is normal can prevent us from placing labels like 'backslider' on ourselves or others as we traverse these difficult transitions in the journey of faith.

The leading writer in this area is James Fowler who describes the journey of maturing faith as a journey through successive stages. Jim is a Christian theologian and a psychologist who for many years worked on developing an understanding of the stages or phases of faith that many people move through in their lifetime. Together the stages form a framework that many people find enormously helpful. Jennifer and William's experience indicates the strength that an understanding of the stages of faith can give. Jennifer and William first heard about Fowler's work on the stages of faith when they were invited to a post-church group.

Jennifer So we got an invitation to go along. And that first meeting a man was speaking on the stages of faith. A lot of it was based on a book by James Fowler. We'd never heard of him, we'd never heard of the stages of faith. And it was just captivating. We just sat there with mouths open thinking, that is us! That's us.

William It was uncanny. I just couldn't believe it. It just expressed where I was at and how I felt. It was amazing.

Jennifer We thought we were off the tracks . . . what we were doing was really quite scary. You know people who do this are backsliding.

And we would have concerns for ourselves spiritually . . . So to hear something called stages of faith, we found that very reassuring.

William To think that someone had actually studied it and written a book on it, meant that we weren't unusual . . . it wasn't even just our generation that was suffering from this. It had actually been going on for years and years. It was, I must say, very encouraging to know.

Fowler's stages now provide the foremost understanding of the journey of faith from a thoroughly researched and academically critiqued perspective. They also form the theoretical base for much current research relating to the internal motivation for people leaving particular types of religious organizations at particular points of their lives.[6]

Of course, what Fowler points to in his stages of faith have been known by generations of Christians. Many of the writings of the Christian saints of old indicate a similar progression of Christian faith involving distinct changes and stages. St Teresa of Avila, in her account of the Christian journey as a progression through different rooms of an interior castle, describes a very similar process to that of Fowler's faith stages. There are more examples in the writings of the Catholic spiritual leaders like St John of the Cross and St Thomas Aquinas. But it isn't only the great Catholic spiritual leaders and psychologists who have written about faith stages. In story form so too did John Bunyan in the classic novel *The Pilgrim's Progress* and Hannah Hurnard in her novel *Hinds' Feet on High Places*.[7] While it does not matter which model we use to provide a context or backdrop for our own journey I am sure an understanding of at least one model is incredibly reassuring, offering both hope beyond present crises and indications of what others have found before us. For our purposes I am briefly going to outline James Fowler's stages of faith as one such model.

For Fowler, faith is a dynamic, changing and evolving process rather than something which is relatively static. For this reason he describes faith as a verb. In normal conversation we think of faith as a noun: something you have or don't have. But Fowler understands faith as a verb, which is a process of becoming. This process of becoming involves our loving, trusting, believing, acting, suffering, valuing, knowing and committing. In this sense faith is more than an acceptance of certain statements of belief – rather it is a way of living which encompasses all of life.

Fowler suggests that as we enter each new stage of faith there is a change in each of the following areas:

1 The way people think.
2 Their ability to see another's point of view.
3 The way they arrive at moral judgements.
4 The way and extent to which they draw boundaries around their faith community.
5 The way they relate to external 'authorities' and their truth-claims.
6 The way they form their world-view.
7 The way they understand and respond to symbols.[8]

Not surprisingly, when we consider the degree of change involved between stages, the transition between stages can be very difficult and traumatic. Although Fowler describes six stages, because of the difficulty and struggle involved in moving from one stage to another very few people progress through all six; many adults only progress through the first two or three. Because of this he is very careful to clarify the fact that no stage is better than another. People who settle at one stage do not have a better faith nor are they more saved than someone who is best described as being at another faith stage. Having said this, there is also a sense in which each successive stage offers a deeper and broader understanding and experience of faith than the stage which precedes it.

If we need to remember that no stage is 'better' than any other we also need to constantly keep in mind that the faith journey Fowler describes is not a gentle, undemanding stroll through life, involving gradual and imperceptible steps. On the contrary, the transitions between stages are often experienced as radical upheavals and major crises. One researcher in this area likens a move from one stage to another to being shipwrecked.

> To undergo shipwreck is to be threatened in a most total and primary way. Shipwreck is the coming apart of what has served as shelter and protection and has held and carried one where one wanted to go – the collapse of a structure that once promised trustworthiness. Likewise, when we undergo the

shipwreck of meaning at the level of faith, we feel threatened at the very core of our existence.[9]

These transitional changes from one stage to another can be very difficult for the person involved and it may seem as though their faith is 'shipwrecked'. This feeling can carry on for long periods of time, sometimes years rather than months. Faith stage transitions are often so difficult, painful and protracted that people often remain locked in a previous stage rather than face the difficulty or uncertainty of the change. In fact, people tend to stay where they are until the pain of staying becomes unbearable. As Alan Jones states:

> It seems to be a maxim of the spiritual life that no-one undergoes spiritual or psychological growth and change *willingly*. We are either dragged into it kicking and screaming, or circumstances force us into the next scene of the human comedy. Ironically the institutional church is often an obstacle to spiritual growth. As we have seen, it has something of an investment in keeping its members in an infantile state.[10]

Let us briefly consider the six stages in the journey of faith that Fowler has researched.

Stage 1: The Innocent[11]

This stage is found in pre-school children whose lives are a seamless world of fantasy, stories, experiences and imagery. Their experience of God and faith is understood through the family experience. Where parents talk about God and pray with the children or say grace, some understanding begins to develop, but at this stage there are no inner structures with which to sort their experiences. Life is therefore a collage of disorganized images including real events of daily life and the imaginary fantasy life of the child.[12]

Stage 2: The Literalist

This stage normally begins when the child is around six years of age. Somewhere around this age the child is better able to organize his or her experiences and begin to categorize them. For literalists, both children and adults, ideas and stories are interpreted literally.

Although powerfully influenced by narrative and story, children at this stage cannot stand back and view events from the position of a neutral observer.

Although this stage begins in childhood, for many this is the stage they settle at during adulthood or at least for a substantial portion of their adulthood. M. Scott Peck, who utilizes a simplified form of Fowler's stages, suggests that from his experience about 20 per cent of the adult population may best be characterized at this stage of faith.[13] Adults at this stage tend to appreciate churches where a more literal interpretation of scripture is encouraged. They are often strongly influenced by rules and authoritative teaching, their main images of God tending to be of a stern, just, but loving parent. Like all the stages there are real strengths to this stage as it offers a strong sense of security for the individual and draws from them deep conviction and commitment.

Stage 3: The Loyalist

This is a conformist stage in which Fowler explains that the individual is 'acutely tuned to the expectations and judgements of significant others'.[14] It is very much a tribal stage, where being part of the tribe is powerfully significant to the person. Here the security of the tribe or community of like-minded believers is important to the individual's own beliefs, values and faith. While loyalists may hold deep convictions and are often committed workers with a very strong sense of loyalty, typically they have not examined their beliefs and values critically. Adults at this stage tend to know what they know but are generally unable to tell you how they know that something is true except by referring to an external authority outside of themselves. The most common example of this is 'The Bible says so', or 'My pastor or church teaches this.'

Predominantly these people have a vision of God as an external, transcendent being and in discussion refer little to God as an immanent in-dwelling God. Perhaps because of this, many are uncomfortable with the notion of the God within.

Among adults this is the stage most commonly found among church members. This should not be surprising, as this is why we have churches and congregations in which people can find some common faith identity, and a community of faith to belong to, where the individual's beliefs, values and actions are shaped. Often identification with their church is a key identity marker for them.

Most find enormous meaning for their faith as they share in the activities of the church – worship, teaching, prayer and mission endeavours. Many experience a strong sense of belonging to their church community which is often expressed as having 'an arrived feel to it', being 'at home' and providing a 'walled-in'[15] commitment. The image of the church community as a large family in which there are strong bonds and friendships is often very appealing. Because of this, conflict and controversy are threatening to them and they will tend to work for harmony, preferring to bury conflict than allow it to surface and potentially destabilize the sense of community which is so important to them.

Stage 4: The Critic

The transition to the fourth stage of faith is probably the most difficult to traverse and involves the greatest dismantling of what was learnt and experienced in the previous stage. Because of the 'walled-in', secure feel of the third stage it often takes a major upset for the transition beyond Stage 3 to begin. Fowler describes the move toward the fourth stage as a two-part transition. The first involves the emergence of a new sense of self that will take responsibility for its own actions, beliefs and values and will stand out against significant others. The second aspect is a new objectification and examination of the beliefs, values and expectations they have received. It is often a very difficult and destabilizing journey.

The critics raise previously accepted beliefs, values, world-views and actions for inspection, often as if they were looking at them and analysing them for the first time. In this critical examination flaws, inconsistencies, unanswered aspects and overly simplistic solutions seem to be their primary focus as they unpick their previous faith, beliefs and practices. It is a lonely, uncomfortable and often protracted affair. But through this process a new respect and trust for one's inner feelings, intuitions and personal judgement is commonly experienced. In contrast to the previous stage, the critic trusts his or her own perception more than the perception and view of any community of others.

At this stage people frequently see themselves as 'self-sufficient, self-starters, self-managing and self-repairing'.[16] Because of the strength of the sense of self and the inner determinancy people at this stage do not sit easily within a leadership structure that requires them to be dependent. They want a leadership structure that acknowledges and respects their personal positions and allows room for them to contribute to the decision-making.

Stage 5: The Seer

This fifth stage encapsulates what may at first seem contradictory aspects. In fact, it is this seeming contradiction which lies at the heart of Stage 5, for at this stage a paradoxical form of understanding is embraced. At this stage the firm boundaries of the previous stage become more porous. The confident self becomes humblingly aware of the depth of the unconscious and the unknown. This is a process which often coincides with a realization of the power and reality of death. Although the transition between stages cannot be fixed to certain ages and people move through at different paces and equilibrate at different points, this stage is seldom reached before the onset of mid-life. Fowler sums up the pre-requisite experience necessary for this stage by saying we have learnt 'by having our noses rubbed in our own finitude'.[17]

Fowler describes this stage by outlining four distinctive hallmarks:

1   An awareness of the need to face and hold together several unmistakable *polar tensions* in one's life: the polarities of being both *old* and *young*, of being both *masculine* and *feminine*, of having a conscious and a shadow self.[18]
2   A felt sense that truth is more multiform and complex than most of the clear, either/or categories of the previous stage. In its richness, ambiguity and multidimensionality, truth must be approached from at least two or more angles of vision simultaneously.[19] Fowler illustrates this point with reference to the 'discovery in physics that to explain the behaviour of light requires two different and irreconcilable models – one based on the model of packets of energy and one on wave theory'.[20] People at this level will resist a forced synthesis or reductionist interpretation and are generally prepared to live with ambiguity, mystery, wonder, and apparent irrationalities.[21]
3   Here faith moves beyond the reductive strategy by which the critic interprets symbol, myth and liturgy into conceptual meanings . . . The faith of the seer gives rise to a second naïveté, a post-critical receptivity and readiness for participation in the reality brought to expression in symbol and myth.[22]

4   A genuine openness to the truths of traditions and communities other than one's own. This openness, however, is not to be equated with a relativistic agnosticism (literally a not knowing), for this stage of faith exhibits a combination of committed belief in and through the particularities of a tradition, while insisting upon the humility that knows that the grasp on ultimate truth that any of our traditions can offer needs continual correction and challenge.[23]

People at this stage love mystery and seem to relish the vastness of the unknown. They are able to identify with perspectives other than their own. Many people best described at this stage of faith have talked to me of a new discovery and appreciation of Catholic expressions of faith, others of gaining much from liberation theology, feminist theology, creation spirituality or aspects of the New Age movement. This does not involve an uncritical or total acceptance of these perspectives; rather it is an acknowledgement and incorporation within their own faith and understanding of a number of new perspectives.

The seer's faith is clearly one's own. Although nurtured by the faith of parents, significant leaders, writers and the lives of others it is the individual's own compilation and one that is deeply held. Their faith may well be quite orthodox, deviating little, if at all, from the faith they previously espoused, or it may relish aspects of faith and ideology from other perspectives. What is significant is that it is the owned and firmly rooted faith of the individual, a faith which shapes and connects with all aspects of their lives.

The boundaries of faith at this stage are often very broad and difficult for others to identify. For this reason people at Stage 5 are often confusing, irritating, even threatening to those at previous stages. As Fowler says, these individuals are 'not likely to be "true believers", in the sense of an undialectical, single-minded, uncritical devotion to a cause or ideology . . . they know that the line between the righteous and the sinners goes through the heart of each of us and our communities, rather than between us and them.'[24]

Stage 6: The Saint
The final stage involves two major transitions: first, what Fowler calls a 'decentration from self', in which the self is removed from the centre or focus of the individual's life. It is a move beyond the

usual human obsessions with survival, security and significance coupled with a continued widening of the circle of 'those who count'. The second transition is a shift in motivation to the complete acceptance of the ultimate authority of God in all aspects of life. This shift is perhaps best illustrated when we observe Jesus in the Garden of Gethsemane: 'Father, if thou art willing, remove this cup from me; nevertheless not my will, but thine, be done.'[25]

Fowler[26] speaks of Mother Teresa, Dietrich Bonhoeffer and Martin Luther King Jr as examples of people who have lived out the rare faith quality encapsulated in this, his final stage of faith.

The stages of faith not only apply to individuals but also to churches. Fowler suggests that as an individual can be described as operating at a particular faith stage, so too can a family, a church or any other group of people. In Fowler's language of faith stages most EPC churches would be best described as operating at a Stage 3 level in terms of their teaching, worshipping patterns, style of governance, leadership and the role models that are typically held up for the congregation to follow. Many leavers and faith strugglers from within such churches would be best described as operating principally from the transition between Stages 3 and 4 on Fowler's list.

It is when there is a major mis-match between the dominant faith stage of a church (or Christian group) and particular individuals that people begin to feel they don't fit, that the church isn't helping them and it is time to move on. For most people the decision to move on comes after much self-blame, repeated attempts to try and 'fit in' and prolonged soul-searching.

We often see a process in people who come to one of the groups we run for people struggling with faith and church issues, in which something, or a succession of things, has occurred to challenge their present stage of faith. With the destruction of this 'way of living out their faith' comes a fundamental shaking which brings with it a continued suspiciousness about God and God's involvement in the details of their lives; even, for some, to the point of wondering whether God exists at all. During this time some flirt with atheism, somewhat like trying on an extreme outfit in a clothing shop, looking at it in the mirror, perhaps for quite a while, as they decide whether atheism really fits them and their total experience of faith. Most often in the end they settle back to a less radical option. Having toyed with atheism and then choosing to pull back from a strong denial of God, despite the very hurt and angry feelings they still carry, some settle for a 'distracted God' – the God who is out there but not really involved in the day-to-day realities of our lives. While these people may concede that God may have set the world turning with inbuilt processes, rhythms and rules, they sense that God has largely left the rest up to us. We are responsible for making our own decisions and finding our own peace. Settling for this view of God is safe – but few find it satisfying. Mostly it is a temporary stance. The internal jury is really still out – keeping options open but watching and still very suspicious. It may be that, like Job, we voice our feelings, doubts and questions to God during this time. We rage against God, vent our anger and disappointment at the loss of the God we thought we had. As Job complained: 'Why did I not perish at birth, and die as I came from the womb?';[27] 'Does it please you to oppress me, to spurn the work of your hands, while you smile on the schemes of the wicked?';[28] 'Show me my offence and my sin. Why do you hide your face and consider me your enemy?'[29]

For some, this position can be followed by a growing sense that God is one who doesn't take away the pain or give neat answers to life's problems. God treats us more like adults and befriends us in the midst of the worst of life and in the midst of us making adult choices and responsibilities. With this can come a metaphorical glimpse of God undergirding what is going on in life and a new sense of the trust that is being called from us. Again Job gives us a glimpse of his own awakening. For even while Job is complaining and questioning, he still goes beyond his feelings and considers again what he knows of God's character. 'To God belong wisdom and power; counsel and understanding are his';[30] . . . 'Even now my witness is in heaven; my advocate is on high. My intercessor is my friend as my eyes pour out tears to God.'[31]

Job weighs up what he knows of God and decides to trust regardless, saying 'Though he slay me, yet will I trust in him.'[32] This was the point Michelle came to, saying:

> *Michelle* What is my faith and who do I believe? I came down to the nuts and bolts and said I do believe . . . I believe him to be good and true and holy and pure and loving . . . at this stage, like Job I had laid my hand on my mouth and am having nothing much to say.

Because he's bigger than I thought he was, I feel I need to get to know him in a much bigger way. Part of my journey now is to accept that I am here. And process my thoughts . . . usually telling him in my musings, thoughts and feelings . . . I feel sobered in my spirit . . . might be grief . . . I've been changed somehow.

The stage of faith that best describes Michelle is the fifth stage – the paradoxical faith of the seer. She came to this new understanding of faith through a long desert experience in which her previously settled understanding of Christian faith was destroyed by suffering and deep questions. Like Job, it was a time of suffering with no answers but a deep personal sense of God leading her to a new way – stage – of Christian faith. Because it is such a destabilizing and painful journey, many people resist the breaking down of a previous stage of faith. J. O. Hagberg and R. A. Guelich point to Jonah as an example of someone who resists all attempts to be moved to a new stage of faith.

> The story of Jonah illustrates a person who has God in a box. Not wanting to accept the fact that his God could care for people different from his type, Jonah jumped ship to avoid adapting. Unfortunately, his flight from reality nearly cost him his life. Faced again with the alternatives, Jonah decided to accept the fact, in theory at least, that God knew neither national or racial boundaries. When the people of Nineveh turned to God, Jonah began to pout because what he had feared had come true. The story ends with him angry at God because God had indeed been gracious with the detestable people of Nineveh. Jonah's anger was so intense that he wished he could die. He was much more comfortable with a provincial view of God who played favourites.[33]

The reality is that we have all lost trust at different times in God and Christian faith – the difference between us is probably only the degree of pain caused by that loss of trust and faith. But such a loss of faith and trust can lead through a confusing and disorienting time into a new 'stage' of faith.

Most of us find the hardest person to forgive and learn to trust again is actually ourselves. The move into the fifth stage of faith requires a new sense of self-forgiveness and humility. We have to be able to forgive ourselves and move beyond bridling ourselves with our own mistrust. I spoke recently with a young woman who spoke of seeing herself in the biblical scene where the Pharisees brought a woman caught in adultery to Jesus. At one and the same time she saw herself as the woman dragged before the crowd – guilty, shamed and embarrassed – and as the last accuser still standing when the others had left. She remained with a stone in hand ready to throw at the guilty woman. How many of us could identify with this same dual characterization? How hard it is to put down the stone we have held ready to throw at ourselves and embrace with care and gentleness the self we hate. This is the long journey to self-respect, care and love. Sadly, without forgiveness there is no future, for from it springs trust beyond suspicion.

Like Peter in the account at the end of John's Gospel, we may need to recognize our own part in the breakdown of our trust in God. Despite his best intentions, Peter denied Jesus three times. Yet Jesus saw beyond that and knew Peter's intentions and entrusted him with new and even greater responsibilities. Like Peter, Job and Michelle, we too are faced with the question, Are we willing to forgive others and be open to trusting again? What is required is not blind trust; we need to work through the issues, finding a trust that may be very cautious at first. When we are hurt we detach, become suspicious and guarded: that is normal. But like the rider who is bucked off, we either get back up and on the horse – albeit that we do so cautiously, carefully, and with our eyes open to potential dangers – or we give up riding. The same is true in the life of faith; in the end, when our bruises are healed and we have had time to catch our breath, we choose to step up or step back. There can be no middle ground. Peter and Michelle have chosen to step up. As Job said, even though God let me down, yet will I still trust him.

10

The Gospel In and Beyond Evangelism

―◆―

Matt and Sally went forward 'to commit their lives to Christ' the first night they went along to church. They had been invited to Matt's brother's place for lunch and after spending the afternoon together they decided to go off to his church in the evening. Although they had both had some prior church experience as children and teenagers it had made little lasting impression on their lives, something that was all about to change:

> *Sally* We went to church that night and it was an amazing experience. Church like we had never known it really. Just the choruses and people worshipping God.

> *Matt* Very charismatic.

> *Sally* They had an altar call and we both went forward and were counselled in a traditional way . . . and we were signed and sealed. We signed the cards and went away. That was the beginning of church life for us.

> *Matt* It radically changed our lives . . . I was a new convert, it had a radical impact on my life. New emotional experiences and life experiences. I loved that period of my life. It was an introduction to a new world and I found it absolutely enthralling at the time and you couldn't keep me away. I would go to two services each Sunday. It was a very exciting time in our lives.

For Matt and Sally this was the start of a journey into the Christian faith that would lead them to an evangelism training course and from there to full-time employment in an evangelistic para-church movement. Soon Matt became the head teacher at the evangelism school and part of the national leadership team. This was a team that he would eventually lead. Matt and Sally were 'long-term' people who remained significantly involved in this para-church group as it grew and developed through the heady days of the Jesus Movement and the Charismatic renewal.

Matt's role meant a lot of travel, teaching, preaching, pro-grammes, leading evangelistic rallies, and building an ever-growing network of trainees and workers. When they later moved to set up a new school they formed links with a new church that was very supportive of their evangelistic work and allowed them to use their facilities regularly.

Sally It was a great relationship we had with this church. We felt supported.

Matt It was wonderful.

Some years later Matt and Sally came to a new crossroads.

Matt In a lot of ways we had been there and done that. We had done everything you could imagine. We had lived in horrific circumstances, with 50 children. We had run schools, we had preached, we had ministered to people, we'd taught, we'd counselled. We had run through all the gamut of things we could do and we had a desire to do some different things. Our thinking had changed radically, particularly in the last five years, and particularly in regard to the Church in the world. Christianity and issues like, our whole thinking about financial matters compared to when we first joined. We were growing older: I was in my mid-thirties, Sally in her early thirties. We started to be more aware of all those things like family. Financial issues became more of an issue, looking ahead, starting to think about planning for your future. Was there going to be more of the same, was there going to be a rosier future, as far as financial things were concerned? I had a great desire to be involved in the business area. I had done teaching, preaching and so on for donkey's years and I was sort of sick of talking. Both of us are very practical people. Both of us like to see things that really work. We haven't got a lot of time for things that are just for their own sake. So it was just time for a change really. It was time to move on. We had probably gone stale, not many people would have recognized that, but internally we were stale.

Underneath the decision to move on and start their own business was a deep reassessment of their Christian faith which eventually led them not only to leave their role as national leaders of the parachurch group but also to leave their church. They became part of a post-church group of similar leavers as they completely reassessed their faith.

In 1995 when I interviewed Sally and Matt they no longer saw a strong need to convert people. Instead they were happy to form close friendships and let the faith stuff 'gently brew in the background without having to be talked about all the time'. As Matt said:

> *Matt* I have been through the whole gambit of teaching, preaching, ministering to people; all that stuff. You know, praying for people and seeing God move. Seeing God move singularly in people and in whole groups; delivering people from demons, inner healing. I would see individuals and then groups of people slayed in the Spirit. Now that's like a huge sack of live kittens to me now and I have put the sack up there on the shelf. I don't know what to do with them. I don't know whether to kill them, drown the lot of them or to let them out again. You know! I don't know what to do with all of that, because a lot of it was extremely real. A lot of it was rubbish. No, not a lot, some of it was rubbish. And a good portion was in the middle. Some was absolutely genuine. Things have happened that I can't explain and could never have engineered or done. It had an incredible impact on people's lives. I can't explain that but somewhere in that mix God is in there.

Seven years later when I went back to find out how faith had changed and moved for them, Matt made it clear that they were still very much people of Christian faith. He said: 'I believe more strongly than ever that God has a real world plan for our life and that as I push into that I will discover God and the real things of life at deeper and more satisfying levels.' When I asked about sharing his faith, he said, 'I want to bring change to the world through expressing my faith in every area I operate in, but after many years of evangelistic endeavour I do not have a desire to proselytize as a main event in my life.' I think I know what he means.

At 14 I went to a youth group camp with a friend. At the camp, despite having been to a Sunday school programme for most of my childhood, I heard for the first time the 'need to make a personal commitment' to Christ. On the last night of the camp there was an opportunity for people to come to the front and 'to ask Jesus to forgive their sins and become Lord of their life'. At the time I was very interested but also not willing to respond publicly in front of my peers. I didn't go forward but slipped one of the small books – a tract – with 'the prayer' at the back of it into my pocket.

That night, back in our room and after I thought my mate Chris was asleep, I knelt up in the old squeaky double bed, found my torch, shone it on the back page of the book inside my sleeping bag, and began to quietly read the prayer. I had at least learnt that you kneel to pray. About half-way through whispering the prayer I heard a voice, clear and audible. 'What are you doing?' It was Chris from the bed across the room. 'Nothing,' I said as I carefully lay back down and waited until I was absolutely certain he was asleep. Later that night I successfully knelt in the old squeaky bed, turned the torch on and whispered the prayer.

I'm not sure what happened that night. Certainly it was nothing tangible or dramatic. There were no voices, visions or strange feelings. But at the end of the camp I did take home a small book of readings based on the Gospel of John with 31 days of notes and readings. For the first time, I wanted to read the Bible and got a lot out of the notes and the way they guided me through the book of John. I don't remember any details of those readings but I do remember they were very important and motivated me in my new Christian faith. For me this was to be the first of many such significant decision points at camps and special services.

Through these key decisions and the slow exploration and growth between them, I came to understand at least something of what it means to be 'Christian' and this became a determining value in my life.

Part of what I believed in, not surprisingly as it was confirmed through my own experience, was an emphasis on evangelism. During the ensuing years I, like Matt and Sally, have done my fair share of evangelism classes, workshops and seminars. In retrospect their underlying theme comes down to a simple 'lifeboat theology'.

From the perspective of a 'lifeboat theology' people are viewed as floating aimlessly in the ocean. The Church is seen as the lifeboat that comes to rescue these sometimes floating, sometimes drowning people from the water. When people make it on to the lifeboat they are, of course, saved from the perils of the ocean. Theologically the image derives from Cyprian, a north African lawyer and ecclesiastical statesman who lived in the third century after Christ. Cyprian defined the Church as the 'ark of salvation', or the community in which one is saved. If the Church is seen in this way – as the ark of salvation – then you need to be in the church lifeboat to be saved. Using this lifeboat image of salvation, certain premises naturally followed:

1 There is a clear division between those in the lifeboat and those in the water, so there is a clear division between the saved and the unsaved, the lost and the saviours.
2 God is seen as being at work in the boat and not at work in the ocean; in fact it is often the devil who is seen as at work there.
3 The basis on which someone is saved or lost is clearly seen. Using the lifeboat image, it is determined by whether or not you are in the boat. In a spiritual sense the decision to get in the boat corresponds to the conscious and decisive act of belief and trust in Jesus as the Son of God, the one who forgives sin.
4 The image provides an intrinsic motivation for helping people get out of the water and into the boat. Christian people who care for others, especially their own loved ones, are strongly motivated to ensure they make it into the lifeboat. The image also carries an inherent sense of guilt for those on the boat who are not otherwise motivated to help sea-dwellers into the boat.

Listening to evangelical Christians speak, I am constantly surprised at the degree to which the 'lifeboat' type of dichotomy shapes people's perceptions and actions when it comes to sharing their faith. But today I find the lifeboat analogy too restrictive. Let's not deny the truth it describes; after all, the image and the premises we have drawn from it encapsulate my own experience of coming to know God and the Christian faith. But I find for myself, and certainly for many of the people I have interviewed who were distancing themselves from evangelical church contexts, that this approach doesn't ring true in the same way it seemed to previously.

A comment from a churchgoer from a newspaper interview can illustrate this feeling:

> Mrs Bell likes the fact that the church encourages people to question and explore their faith. She's always open about being a churchgoer; but she's not into converting others. 'I prefer to encourage people rather than try to convert them by standing on a soapbox.'[1]

When I went back to the church leavers, like Matt and Sally, and asked them about how their faith had moved and changed in the ensuing five-plus years, one of the recurring themes was their re-evaluation of their view of evangelism. For many, this perspective on how people come to Christian faith is simply redundant, unhelpful, and far too limiting. Listening to these leavers, questioning people in the Church, and my own struggling, it seems my perspective has changed and a fundamental re-evaluation has occurred. But why?

The first funeral I was involved in as a minister was of an 80-year-old plumber whom I had only ever met once in the early hours of the morning as he lay dying and unconscious in hospital. The next day he died and I went to visit his widow to prepare for the funeral. Listening to his wife, I learnt that he was not a religious man. He never went to church, never talked about God or read the Bible, but he was a good man. He ran a small plumbing business in which he was always honest and reliable, fair and hard-working. He had been a good family man and a loving husband for nearly 60 years. When we talked about the service there were no hymns, readings or prayers that he would have wanted or particularly liked. I left feeling stuck as to how to approach this man's funeral, but also bewildered by one detail that his wife had told me. As we talked she had described a ritual her husband had every night of their marriage. He would climb into bed at night, lie on his back and for ten minutes or so he would pray. His wife knew not to talk to him for these first few minutes in bed as he prayed. In my clear-minded evangelicalism I didn't know where to place this man. Put simply, was he saved and going to heaven, or was he simply a good man who died unsaved? What would I say at the funeral?

When we read the words of Jesus regarding who is 'saved' and who is 'lost' we come to see that things aren't as clear-cut as the

121

lifeboat image leads us to believe. For example, Jesus' teaching talks about weeds in the good crop,[2] goats in the flock[3] and people who claimed to know Jesus but really don't know him at all.[4] In other words there are people who look like they are 'in' who really are not. Equally Jesus taught that the sinners, tax collectors, prostitutes,[5] children[6] and the lowest of the low[7] who saw themselves, and were seen by others, as outcasts are in fact included in the 'kingdom of heaven'. Now when you have weeds in the crop, goats in the flock and sinners, children and outcasts in the kingdom it becomes increasingly clear that the simple boundaries of who is in and who is out don't hold. At least not the way Jesus saw things.

> *Matt* I could never accept that God was going to send so many people to hell . . . The vast majority are going to go to hell. I just couldn't accept that. There was no way, in my sense of fairness, that a loving God could do that.

Alan Jones, Dean of Grace Cathedral in San Francisco, takes Matt's view further:

> Our choices are critical, but I find no grounds for believing that the process of our making claims and living them through is irrevocably settled at death. God is just and life is sometimes 'hell', but to insist, as many do, that a person is damned everlastingly if he or she fails to make a personal, verbal commitment to Jesus Christ, is both absurd and morally repellent. What about all those who haven't made a decision for Jesus Christ because of the terrible example of those who have? Are we believers not implicated in their damnation?[8]

His way of believing:

> Hopes for the salvation of everyone and of all things; and, while it allows for the terrible mystery and possibility of someone being lost and saying 'No' to the movement of life and love in the heart, it resists making a judgement with regard to the end of those 'whose faith is known to God alone'. It believes and trusts in the working of the Holy Spirit in all human beings.[9]

In some cases it would seem believers have an almost perverse attraction to the idea of personal damnation, not for themselves of course but for others they know. Jones on the other hand suggests an alternative:

> I am puzzled why the doctrine of eternal punishment is still revered by so many Christians. It cannot be explained simply as a desire to preserve human freedom, although I suppose it must be logically possible for a person to go on saying 'No' to God for ever. Christian orthodoxy requires that I believe in the logical possibility of hell (utter lostness and damnation). It does not require that I believe anyone is there. There is nothing to prevent my hoping that hell is empty.[10]

If the boundaries between who is saved and who isn't are not so clear, neither are the boundaries between where God is at work and where God isn't at work. Recently I've read two books by Paul Hawker, a successful TV documentary maker, who left his career to search for deeper meaning in his own life. His first book[11] describes a 40-day pilgrimage taken on his own in an isolated mountain range. Staying away from other hikers as much as possible he spent these 40 days alone with the mountains, the views, the birds and God. The book is a very moving account of a man finding God speaking to him and leading him to some profound personal revelations. Hawker's second book[12] focuses on the times when God breaks through into our lives in a whole variety of ways. Bringing together the fruit of research projects including those of Sir Alister Hardy and David Hay with the anecdotal accounts of many people he has discussed faith with, he shows that encounters with the supernatural and God are not unusual and certainly not confined to 'Christians'.

Drawing on David Hay's research in the United Kingdom, Hawker showed that when people are asked in a safe and value-free environment most are willing to describe deeply moving spiritual experiences. But few are willing to talk about them in general conversation. As one middle-aged factory worker put it, 'No, I've not told anyone. For the simple reason, there's such a lot of disbelievers about and they'd ridicule you.' Another described his own silence saying, 'I'd tell the wife. I don't tell me mates, otherwise they'd think I'd gone barmy.' These spiritual experiences outside the Christian networks appear to concur with the way Jesus worked. He too spent a great deal of his time outside the religious establishments and structures, talking with and meeting people in the markets, by the road or where groups of people gathered. And he taught in a way that reflects the view that God is at work beyond the religious structures.[13]

Possibly you too are sensing that things aren't as clear-cut as the evangelical lifeboat image leads us to believe. There are people in the lifeboats who aren't followers of Christ and people in the water who are, and God seems to be very much at work in the lives of those in the water as well as those in the boats. This leads us to the third premise of the analogy; that a conscious and decisive act of belief and trust in Jesus is required to move from the water (the lost) into the boat (to become one of the saved). Yet if we put this premise under closer scrutiny we find it too is hard to defend. Recently I heard a woman who works with severely intellectually handicapped children answer a friend's question as to whether any of the children she worked with were Christians. The woman's reply was quite adamant – 'Yes, they are.' Many of them couldn't speak or communicate and they understood very little of what was going on around them, but they were, in this woman's eyes, 'deeply spiritual people'. Yet clearly few, if any, of these children will ever be able to make the kind of conscious and deliberate decision that I was able to make as a 14-year-old on camp.

Of course evangelical theologians have made exceptions for children like those I've described and for babies, the intellectually handicapped, people who never hear the call to conversion and people whose life's circumstances have placed serious and insurmountable barriers in the way of making such a decision. But I wonder if all the exceptions to the rule don't mean we need to reassess the rule. Greatest among these exceptions is what happens to all the people of other faiths and philosophies who do not convert to the Christian faith? Are they simply fodder for the fires of hell? If so, what does this say about the character and nature of the God being proclaimed?

This is especially so when we consider the greater understanding we now have about culture and faith. So much of the faith that people have is shaped by the cultural context in which they are brought up. Therefore the birthplace of thousands of millions of people strongly shapes their faith and beliefs, which inhibits them ever making the kind of conscious choice for Christ that this 'decisionism' requires. The issue of what happens to people of other faiths is one with which the Catholic Church has also had to grapple – with surprising results. Hans Küng explains that included in Vatican II 'was a new, constructive attitude towards Islam and the other world religions. It was recognised that in principle salvation is also possible outside Christianity, even for atheists and agnostics, if they act in accordance with their conscience.'[14]

A careful reading of the Gospels shows that Jesus in fact related to each person in decidedly unique ways and didn't try to encourage people to do the same thing as their neighbour. To some, Jesus focused on their physical health and incorporated this into their spiritual forgiveness; to others he said 'Leave something'; to one (but only one!) he said, 'You must be born again.' To another who hung on the cross beside him he said, 'You will be with me in paradise.' To a woman who touched him he said, 'Don't worry! You are now well because of your faith.'[15] To the religious leaders he said, 'If you don't change and become like a child, you will never get into the kingdom of heaven.'[16]

To distil the ways Jesus related to individual people in the scriptures down to one way of coming to know God is simply too narrow. I realize that Jesus spoke about the narrow way and the wide highway, but are we to believe that this was meant as a restriction on the avenues through which people could come to know God rather than a comment about the difficulty of setting a course after God?

Having discussed the first three premises of salvation based on the lifeboat imagery, I want to suggest that in each case things are not as black and white or clear-cut as the image implies. Who is in and who is out is more fuzzy than the image depicts; God is very much at work in the lives of people in the ocean as well as the boat, and the concept of a conscious definitive decision being the only rope ladder to the lifeboat is seriously problematic. This doesn't mean the lifeboat image needs to be discarded, but it does mean things are nowhere near as clear-cut as the image may have led us to believe. This leads us to the final premise of the lifeboat analogy; that it is a powerful motivator for evangelism. If we accept that the faith lives of people are more complex and unique, then, some would claim, it removes the rationale for sharing the gospel and calling people to Christ, particularly if we couple this with the notion that eternal decisions are God's decisions and are transacted with each individual uniquely.

Many would argue that what is suggested here takes away all motivation for sharing the Christian faith. But does it? Are we only interested in sharing our faith so people get 'saved' and go to heaven? Is the Christian faith only about after-death possibilities? Is there no point in connecting with Christ in the here and now? Surely living in tune with God is important now. Surely coming to know Christ personally is the most significant, liberating and life-giving encounter that anyone can have. Living with a greater understanding of God and room for God to be involved in our lives is better than living with a limited knowledge and with a lesser degree of encounter with God. Surely this is motivation enough for anyone who has found something life-giving in the Christian faith to talk openly about it with others, but without the guilt and the agenda of 'witnessing'.

Paul Hawker sums up the experience of ordinary people of witnessing Christians, saying:

> We've probably shared workplaces and lecture halls with such people, been accosted by them on the streets, found them knocking on our doors, had impassioned relatives and once close friends break every Christian principle they claim to believe in, simply to make a point. A work colleague once confided to me that he didn't like 'fish people', the nickname he gave proselytising Christians because of their fish-shaped bumper stickers. His disdain for them centred around his sister's attempts over two years to get him to convert and join her church. He'd only managed to stop her constant harassment by refusing to visit and forbidding her to visit him. He was quite hurt and embittered by the whole affair.[17]

To return to the Gospels again, Jesus seemed very different from the portrayal of the present-day followers described by Hawker. In contrast, Jesus was concerned about the immediate needs of the people he met. Sometimes he linked these with spiritual needs but often he simply dealt with the presenting illness, question or desire. Even when he sent out the Twelve, his instructions were focused on the presenting needs of the people they would meet – 'Heal the sick, raise the dead to life, heal people who have leprosy, and force out demons. You received without paying, now give without being paid.'[18] Jesus' style treated people as people, not projects to get from A to B or as if they needed to be convinced to buy a particular product. He was able to respect them as people and respect their journey with God and to incorporate that into their present needs and situation.

Clearly another model of salvation that overcomes the inadequacies of the lifeboat analogy is required. Not a bounded set analogy where people are seen as being either in or out but a centred-set analogy that encourages people to consider in which direction they are moving. Are they moving towards the centre or away from it rather than encouraging people to spend their time trying to determine whether they or others are in or out?

The theologian and spiritual director Sheila Pritchard, drawing on the work of Paul Hiebert, a missiologist from Trinity Evangelical School of Divinity, says, 'Centred sets are created by defining a centre and the relationship of people to that centre. All those attached to the centre and moving towards it are members of the set. All those moving away from the centre are not members of the set', regardless, I would want to add, of their relative distances from the centre. Pritchard continues:

> It is much more realistic and helpful to think of Christianity as a centred set: a set defined by movement towards the centre, the person of Jesus Christ. Conversion is the point at which a person turns towards the centre and begins the journey. That new fragile follower of Jesus (about whom we may know very little) is as much a part of the set as the missionary who told him the gospel story. The fact that the missionary has a degree in theology is irrelevant to defining the set. The fact that they are both moving towards the centre goal is what matters.[19]

This is a much more dynamic view of following Christ in which Christ-likeness is emphasized and boundary crossing de-emphasized. Pritchard explains the two sets using an example drawn from Australian cattle ranching. In some areas of Australia large sections of land go for mile after mile without any sign of fences. A visitor, intrigued at how farming cattle was possible without fences, asked a local farmer who explained, 'Oh, that's no problem. Out here we dig wells instead of building fences.' The implication, Pritchard says, is obvious: 'There is no need to fence cattle in when they are highly motivated to stay within range of their source of life.' What we need in our approach to evangelism is far more emphasis on wells and far less on fences. Getting people to climb over fences is not the issue. Being drawn by Christ is.

This is the approach Paul uses when he spoke in Athens. Athens was a very spiritual and learned city, so he said to them: 'People of Athens, I see that you are very religious. As I was going through your city and looking at the things you worship, I found an altar with the words, "To an Unknown God". You worship this God, but you don't really know him.'[20] Perhaps the reactions and new understandings of Maxwell, Jennifer and Matt will help us to see other possibilities for expressing our faith with others:

Maxwell When I was involved with a group of evangelists, I felt so awful about how they would trample over people not caring who the people were. They just wanted another head . . . so I've been scared off evangelism. I don't share unless people provide the opening. I've made two good friends who aren't Christians but we talk about God a lot. They ask me what I believe. I just tell them what I believe and where I'm at. I'm much happier with that than I ever was.

Jennifer We don't have to feel apologetic or defensive for what we believe, and I am quite happy to discuss what I believe and don't believe, where once, in the church, I wouldn't have. Often my motivation I think was wrong. To witness, whereas now it is just people I enjoy being with. I'm happy to sit down and discuss my beliefs but with no pressure on. Basically it is their choice to think different to us, and I feel quite accepting of someone else's beliefs. That can create the guilt feelings again, in terms of being more accepting where a traditional Christian would be a little more narrow. My definition of Christianity has widened, as to who I think may be in heaven, and I feel a bit guilty about that because it is a lot looser than it used to be. And I'm a lot more comfortable with that. I'm not sure where I set my beliefs now. I'm probably a lot more accepting of people who say they believe but don't go to church.

Matt My faith is just who I am, so my involvement with others is an expression of who I am. Both my business partners and I try to have our company act in a manner that reflects our value system regarding

ethics, transparency in our dealings, generosity, employee relationships, customers, social needs and how we operate as a business.
This includes what we produce and its impact on society etc. . . .
My sense of mission has to do with contribution to the world rather
than conversion of it.

11

Commitment to People and the World In and Beyond Mission

◦

I will not live an unlived life,
I will not go in fear
Of falling or catching fire.
I choose to inhabit my days,
To allow my living to open to me,
To make me less afraid,
More accessible,
To loosen my heart
Until it becomes a wing,
A torch, a promise.
I choose to risk my significance:
To live.
So that which came to me as a seed,
Goes to the next as a blossom,
And that which came to me as a blossom,
Goes on as a fruit.

(Davna Markova)[1]

Sacred sites, those places where the barrier between this world and God's presence are very thin, are all unique. As God deals in our lives uniquely the locations of God's encounters with us are also unique. Some sacred sites are deeply personal, a place where we as individuals have been close to God. Others are communal, places of prayer and retreat, cathedrals, sites of human struggle and often sites of great pain. Visiting Ground Zero a year after the destruction of the twin towers, as America and New York remembered 11 September 2001, was for me such a site. Here the sheer cost in human suffering, loss of life and grief meant this was a heavy place. Heavy with a sense of loss and suffering but also heavy with stories of courage, sacrifice and the very best of the human spirit.

Sacred sites like Ground Zero are corporate, others are deeply personal. Personally sacred sites are places where we individually have encountered God, or what we have taken to be God's leading or voice. While we can never prove the divine presence, the impact of these incidents invariably shapes our lives and frames our future direction.

Recently I returned to a very personal sacred site. It is a beautiful place, simply and ruggedly beautiful. A small, isolated bay where the sea is often as still and clear as a mirror. The early mornings can be so calm, and so quiet that it is almost eerie. It was eight years since I had been sitting on the grass under this same tree. It had been early in the morning that I had watched the water, when all was still and calm, within and without, and 'felt' a sense of the divine helping me make a big decision. Eight years on I could reflect on that decision, where it had taken me and how my life had changed because of it. Had it been a 'good decision'? Was it a mistake? Was God a part of it?

For many people that personal sacred site, although attractive and restful, would carry none of the significance it does for me. I long to go back, hopefully before another eight years pass.

It must have been on one of these personal sacred sites that Peter met Jesus in John 21. We are told they were by the Sea of Galilee,[2] again Peter had just been fishing and the fishing boats and gear were around him on the beach. For it was on the beach by the Sea of Galilee that Peter and the other disciples had first met Jesus;[3] then too they had just been fishing.

This second conversation is set at a personally sacred site with triggers that could not help but capture Peter's attention. The beach scene, the vast catch of fish, the warmth from the hot coals on Peter's cold body (remember the last fire recorded in John's Gospel was the fire that the then cold Peter stood around as he denied Jesus three times[4]), Jesus' use of his family name – Simon son of John (which must have taken him back to his fishing days with his brother and father) – must have all struck with deep personal poignancy. This sacred site and the coming of Jesus in ways that carried so many memories set the scene for the conversation that would follow.

The Christ speaking to Peter was and wasn't the same Christ he had followed from the side of this sea three years before. That Christ was flesh and blood. This Christ was now mysterious, other worldly and intangible. Jesus has profoundly changed, but so too would his call to Peter. First time round he was asking Peter to 'follow him'. Years before when Jesus asked Peter this question his answer was immediate. This time it was not so easy. Three years of following Jesus, seeing what his lifestyle and demands were really like, ensured this was no light decision.

As Jesus asked the question, he challenged Peter's own sense of being in control and his sense of knowing what should happen next. Earlier Jesus had said to Peter that he didn't really know what Jesus was doing but that later he would understand. Now that time had come.⁵ As Jesus asked again, 'Peter do you love me?' Peter answered with a new self-awareness and humility, saying to Jesus, 'You know everything.'⁶ Gone was the self-confident, self-assured Peter who felt he knew the best way forward. Peter didn't know any less than he had previously done but he now knew how little knowledge and wisdom he really had. His best wisdom had led him to fail Jesus and lie about his sense of trust and identification with Jesus. Now he was being asked to recognize that shift and own his frailty, limited knowledge and personal weaknesses.

During the conversation Jesus asked Peter, 'Do you love me?' three times. Obviously a painful reminder of the three times Peter had earlier denied Jesus when the young woman asked if he knew this Jesus who was then on trial. Having now brought Peter to this crucial point, Jesus asked not 'Will you follow me?' but 'Do you love me?' This was not some sappy, feel-good, chorus kind of love. It was not even a love that would be personally costly, although that is clearly part of the picture. But it was the kind of love that asks, 'Will you pour out your life for others?' Specifically, 'Will you take responsibility for feeding my lambs?' In biblical imagery it implies, 'Will you teach and care for new followers of mine?' When Jesus asked a second time, he asked 'Will you feed my sheep?' In other words, 'Will you teach and support the faith of my mature followers?' 'Peter, will you provide the depth of prayer and care that long-term followers after God sometimes need?'

This is a big ask. No longer are we talking about fishing boats and a few nets that Peter is asked to leave, but something greater. Jesus is inviting Peter to take far more responsibility and leadership.

It is one thing to leave the old life behind in a flush of enthusiasm and idealism. But those hazy-eyed days are now gone. Peter was being asked to do much more: to commit himself to the care, support and nurture of these other followers. These two calls recorded by the Gospel writers are light years apart. One of the pastoral descriptions given to Jesus is that of the shepherd who loves his sheep. Could it be that Jesus was actually saying to Peter, 'I want you to take my role'? Through this second call, Jesus at once affirmed Peter and said, 'I am willing to trust you with the greatest task there is', a task that Jesus himself had undertaken. Here Jesus was going way beyond simply reinstating Peter or even forgiving him. He was saying to Peter, 'In your confusion and failure you don't even trust yourself but I trust you. I believe in you.'

This is a remarkable calling. After all Peter had said and done, here was Jesus trusting him, reinstating him, believing in him, caring for him and being willing to offer him such an important task: the task that up until this moment Jesus had himself carried.

If this is true for Peter, could it also be true for us as well? Can we too in our own deserts or dark nights of the soul meet with God in a profoundly personal way, as Peter does with Jesus in this chapter of John's Gospel? Do we also sense that God believes in us? That God trusts us? That God is willing to entrust us with a task of eternal gravity? In all our own unique mix of failure, despair, confusion, questions, doubts, tears, grief and pain, could God call us beyond a simple naïvety of faith, beyond a destruction and deconstruction of faith to a new place? A place where God shapes a new faith within us and calls us to love and care for people as Jesus himself did?

We can understand Peter's reluctance. His self-confidence had been eroded. Where he believed he was at his strongest he had failed. What seemed so certain and solid a few weeks earlier had crumbled. Now he was much more reluctant, hesitant, uncertain – even fearful. His inadequacies were now very public and his anxieties about the future and how he could offer anything loom much larger.

Nor could he simply go back as if the last three years, and especially the last few weeks, had never happened. It is the same sea side but the call was now quite different and far more demanding. When Jesus first called, it was to an unknown adventure, and Peter was initially free to believe that Jesus would fulfil all his conscious and unconscious expectations and dreams. However, since Jesus' cross and Peter's conversation round the fire, that had all gone. The real Jesus and his real role were now blatantly evident. It is this Jesus, the crucified and mystical one, who asked Peter not simply to follow him, but to love and care for the people Jesus loved and cared for. This is not the old call restated. Too much water, as they say, had now passed under the bridge. This was a new and more demanding call beyond the naïvety of a pre-Jerusalem faith. It was not an old call and faith reclaimed, but a completely new demanding and risky call.

Peter's only options were to stay where he is, go back fishing and assign the past to the scrapbook of life's memories, or to go on taking up the challenge that Jesus laid before him. The same challenge was laid before Jeremiah. He was initially called as a teenager but then a decade or more later while going through a really dark patch, he was called again. God spoke to him saying,

> If you have raced with men on foot
> > and they have worn you out,
> > how can you compete with horses?
> If you stumble in safe country,
> > how will you manage in the thickets by the Jordan?[7]

He had been put in stocks, had had to flee an angry King and had been lowered into a cistern of mire where his death was almost certain. Now tired, rejected, hurt and disappointed, Jeremiah heard God speaking to him renewing his call and effectively saying, 'Cheer up, Jeremiah, there's worse to come.' He went on slugging it out for 40 years or more.

When this second call came it was a greatly changed Peter and Jeremiah to whom it was given. The pre-Jerusalem Peter could not have loved Jesus' followers. Too full of his own self-confidence, independence, strength and ideas, he needed to go through his own personal desert to be ready for this second call. So too, with each of us, because who we are changes through the experience of darkness and desert. It is because of these changes that we too can be called to the huge responsibility of loving Christ's people. It would be easier to say, 'No. I'm struggling enough on my own. I'm too aware of my own weaknesses, failures and limitations to take on the care of others.' Yet this, I believe, is what God will inevitably call us to. For it is only in the giving and care of others that we ourselves are taken on. The way through the desert is somehow tied to our care of others. In Erickson's terminology it is the call to generativity, generativity at personal cost.

This is the experience of Job. When he had spent his anger and questions on God he was surprisingly encountered by God in a new way. God gave him a new perspective. He was taken to see the creation, the making of the universe, the animals of the deep, and this changed his perspective of himself, of God and of his suffering. He was not given an answer to his questions; the riddle of suffering was not solved, nor even addressed. But as Paul Ricoeur states:

> The God who addresses Job out of the tempest shows him Behemoth and Leviathan, the hippopotamus and the crocodile, vestiges of the chaos that has been overcome, representing a brutality dominated and overcome by the creative act. Through these symbols he gives him to understand that all is order, measure and beauty – inscrutable order, measure beyond measure, terrible beauty.[8]

This new encounter with God changed Job's perspective as he experienced a universe of 'inscrutable order, measure beyond measure and terrible beauty'. The realm of the mysteries of God was entered. It was as though God was speaking a new language to Job, and the old seemed simplistic babbling in the wake of the new. His relationship with God changed: 'My ears had heard of you, but now my eyes have seen you,'[9] he said. Job was humbled by this experience; left only to put his hand over his mouth,[10] for God is much bigger than he had previously appreciated. With this humbling came a softening within him.

This was a major shift for Job. Now instead of arguing with his companions who had spent chapters trying to tell him his sickness and destitution is all his own fault, Job chose to pray for them. He didn't try to rub his friends' noses in their wrong or remind them of their aggressiveness towards him, but was free to pray for them and care for them.

His softening and new inclusiveness were also hinted at in the final section of the book, where only the names of his daughters are mentioned and to whom, with his sons, he gave an inheritance. He gave this to his daughters despite the Old Testament teaching of Numbers 27 where daughters were only entitled to receive an inheritance if there were no sons.

This is the journey of many characters of scripture – Jeremiah, Job and Peter we have already considered, but there is also David beyond the cave, Abraham beyond his many desert wanderings, Moses called back to his own people, the people of Israel through the desert and again beyond the exile of Babylon. And this is many people's journey. The details are always unique yet the flow has similarities. God calls again. God calls in the midst of our personal desert and darkness.

After asking Peter three times if he loved him and calling him to care for and feed his lambs and sheep. Jesus explained what lay ahead of him. It is not a pretty sight. Peter, who had always been independent and strong, was told that one day independence will be taken from him; that when he grew old someone else would dress him and lead him where he did not want to go until finally he would die. Jesus' call is not to a life of ease, comfort or pleasure. No one could blame Peter if he chose to stay by the sea and spend his life fishing, but this was the second call; like Jeremiah's call to go beyond what he could do himself. Jesus ends, after all this, with the familiar words, 'Follow me!'[11] Will you follow me?

The tale and the accounts of biblical characters described above suggest a common feature in the second call of God: this call that we long for in the deserts of criticism, despair and doubt. The common feature is the call to give to and care for others. Hidden in this call is our own growth, fulfilment and healing. It is not an easy call. No one could describe what Peter is called to as easy street. Nor is it a calling that we simply say 'Yes' to and move on. This is a way of life. His answer is biography writ large. A giving of himself in the love of others. Not naïvely or in self-destructive ways, but a giving to others out of our vulnerability and in our weaknesses. A giving that allows God to work deeply.

To bring this chapter to a close I want to turn to scripture for one more story, one more image to guide our thoughts, and then end with an old Hasidic tale and a prayer. Genesis[12] describes Abram's encounter with God in the desert. The issue at stake is that Abram has no descendants. No one will inherit the promises he has received from God. God entices Abram outside the tent to see the night sky, telling him he will have as many descendants as the stars

in the sky above.[13] When Abram later asks how he will know that
God will come through on his promises, God tells him to prepare
an unusual collection of halved animals. Then in 'a thick and
dreadful darkness', God outlines something of the future for
Abram and his descendants long after his death. Like the depiction
Jesus gives Peter, it is not all good news, but within it God's call
and promise are assured. Like Abram, the question that we too
must consider is whether we will have descendants: not children in
our own line but descendants in faith and life. Will we love and
care for others in such a way that they become descendants? People
to whom and through whom the lessons of faith we have learned
are passed on and the richness of our experience of God's presence
and God's absence is carried? The call of Micah sums it up:

> And what does the Lord require of you?
> To act justly and to love mercy
> and to walk humbly with your God.[14]

Now to the Hasidic tale and the prayer.

> 'How can we determine the hour or dawn, when the night
> ends and the day begins?' asked the teacher. 'When from a
> distance you can distinguish between a dog and a sheep?'
> suggested one of the students.
> 'No,' was the answer.
> 'Is it when one can distinguish between a fig tree and a
> grapevine?' asked a second student.
> 'No.'
> 'Please tell us the answer then.'
> 'It is,' said the wise teacher, 'when you can look in the face
> of a human being and you have enough light to recognize in
> him/her your brother/sister. Up till then it is night and darkness
> is still with us.'[15]

> May the Spirit
> Bless you with discomfort
> At easy answers, half-truths and
> Superficial relationships so that
> You will live deep in your heart.

May the Spirit
Bless you with anger
At injustice and oppression,
And exploitation of people and the earth
So that you will work for
Justice, equity and peace.

May the Spirit
Bless you with tears to shed
For those who suffer
So that you will
Reach out your hand
To comfort them.

And may the Spirit
Bless you with the foolishness
To think you can make a difference
In the world,
So you will do the things
Which others say cannot be done.[16]

12

Belonging In and Beyond the Church

———◄○►———

I believe I am called to a mature independence which enables authentic community.[1]

Anne-Marie After a couple of years I joined a group of young people trying to pursue their faith outside the confines of church. When I first left church I had no idea there was a growing number of people doing the same thing, for different reasons, but all trying to maintain a relationship with God while coming to terms with issues surrounding Church and faith. It was useful to be able to talk about things with other people who were also questioning aspects of God and of the Christianity they had been taught to believe. I never talked about the suicide though. It was too painful and too personal.

Even more valuable to me over this time was being able to talk with someone about all of it. Not just the big questions about God but also the horror and sense of abandonment that was the cause of it all. A person I trusted and came to highly respect, and who freely gave me their time on a regular basis. This church figure gave me the freedom to say what I needed to say without judging and without trying to provide all the answers. Without suggesting I needed to return to church in order to find what I was looking for, they provided options and caused me to think about things in new and different ways.

Now nearly five years later, I do sometimes go to church. But I still find it hard. I am still wary of prayer and I still struggle to draw from the Bible anything I can cling to with the kind of certainty I once believed came from placing my life in God's hands. I still get angry at God and I still ache for the loss of a life that had so much promise. But somehow I think more than ever, I believe in a God who above all else is utterly loving. And that provides a more com-

pelling reason than anything else I can think of for pursuing a relationship with God in the face of doubt.

Leaving a community of faith that has been very important to us is
always very difficult. With the leaving comes a sense of loss, loneliness, even aloneness. But compelling reasons drive people to leave
their church, their para-church group or home church. If this
leaving and being alone is difficult, the alternative, re-connecting
with others, is harder. I often wonder how many people have left
churches and Christian groups and still have no face-to-face
contact with any grouping of Christian people where their lives are
honestly shared and their faith by one means or another is encouraged.

Of the hundreds of leavers I have met and talked with the vast
majority have spoken about missing the sense of community and
belonging that they once enjoyed in their church context. The
church was for many years their place of belonging. It provided a
group that reinforced and validated their sense of faith identity. It
provided a community where people at least to some extent knew
each other, were aware of each other's ups and downs and in which
there was some degree of friendship and care. After leaving, many
long for a new place to belong – a new faith community. In order
to meet this need some form, or link up with, faith groups outside
the institutional church structures. Although these EPC church
leavers are abandoning their institutional Church, the majority are
still keen to meet with others who are travelling a similar faith
journey – if they can find them. What most are not willing to do is
be sucked back into a church community that will not accept and
endorse their faith struggles, questions, doubts, despair and loss.
To do so is to lose or invalidate their growing edge.

In this chapter we will look at some of the new forms of
Christian community that are informally appearing alongside and
in some cases within institutional church structures and then move
from there to ask if such groups indicate new ways of structuring
Christian belonging.

When I originally researched the faith of church leavers I was
surprised to find that most (65 per cent) of the people interviewed went on to form or find post-church groups in which they
could belong and share their faith. The role of these post-church
groups varied considerably. Some functioned as gatherings of the

discontented in the process of leaving the church, others as discussion groups primarily focused on concerns that were not
given space in the EPC church environments, while still others
were attempts to be Church for those who have left the institutional churches. These variations are summed up in the
comments of Jill, Sarah and James.

> *Jill* People come to our group because they need a venue where they
> can share more openly and honestly. I was one of those people.

> *Sarah* I felt that church was negatively impacting my relationship
> with God. I really tried hard to see how I could change to make my
> church experience more positive but it didn't work that way. I began
> learning about other ways to relate to God besides those I had been
> taught at my church and found they fitted much more with who I
> am. My church did not seem to allow the kind of emotional reality
> that I was experiencing during a particularly painful episode in my
> life. Church was like a box into which I no longer fitted.

> *James* Once we decided to leave our church it was easy to go. We
> have never missed it. We almost felt like we had outgrown it. It
> seemed that in church we were eternally covering the same ground.

What are these post-church groups like? Why do some church
leavers have such strong attachments to their respective groups?
And what can the institutional churches learn from the emerging
post-church groupings? To help answer some of these questions we
will look at how one of these groups functions, using the notes
Jenny McIntosh made after visiting such a group in action. Jenny
facilitates groups for church leavers and people struggling to make
sense of their faith. She wrote:

> I was met at the door by one of the children of the host family
> and taken into the living room to meet others who had also
> arrived early. Everyone was very friendly and welcoming; they
> seemed very at ease in each other's company, yet also happy and
> relaxed about my presence as a visitor. Food was already
> cooking in the kitchen and others brought more as they arrived.
> Slowly the room was filling with people as the table was
> filling with plates and food ready for brunch together. Over the

next half hour spiders[2] were made for the children while the adults chatted and caught up on each other's news. Conversations ranged over various everyday events including the political news, international and local sport; even the local schoolboy teams in which some of the children in the group played, were topics of conversation by parents who were obviously faithful supporters. The children seemed to move easily in and out of these conversations and their own games. Clearly they too were an important part of the group and were obviously very relaxed in this atmosphere. Then the conversation shifted with new concern and care as one group member explained how a friend had died in tragic circumstances that week. People acknowledged in genuine ways the struggle it must be coming to terms with this loss.

When everyone had arrived the food was laid out on the table. The meal was not simply a formality or a pre-cursor to the group time but a very integral part of what they seemed to share together. Time was taken over their food and people chatted, socialized and ate as the children came in and out for plates of food in between playing games or watching a video together in an adjoining room.

After lunch Simon, one of the group members and facilitator of the day's discussion, got everyone's attention and asked people to take a seat. He began with a couple of word pictures and then showed two original modern paintings. The paintings were used to challenge people's assumptions regarding the meaning we take from what we see; and how we connect what we see into our prior experience. Drawing on the group's knowledge and experience, as well as a reading from a book on the wisdom of the soul, he slowly guided us toward the points he hoped the group would find. He wanted us to see that we need to give ourselves time and space in order to see what is beyond the immediate. We need to really get in 'behind' what we see, like Jesus did, if we are to see beyond the immediate and the taken for granted.

Although the Bible was not explicitly used, group members' contributions included direct and indirect references to specific biblical passages and stories. Clearly these people knew the scriptures well, and they were used to connecting the biblical narratives with their own stories and experiences.

While members of the group take turns at leading, there is no appointed leader. A couple of people do, however, provide, what they call, the 'glue' of the group; ensuring that matters of basic organization and communication are covered and giving some energy to group life. Talking to people after the discussion you quickly realize how important the group is to them. It provided strong friendships and there were very close links among the group members. One couple spoke to me about how they were feeling very supported by the group through a recent difficult personal time.

Speaking about what had attracted them to the group, people mentioned a variety of factors, among them: the intimacy, feeling that they were being heard, the humour in the group and the feeling of safety the group provided. Others said that this was a place where they could be themselves with no pressure to have to be something different. That there was a sense of freedom from having to pretend combined with genuine support and acceptance for people as they took the time they needed to heal. Still others said the fact that they had a shared history with other group members was important to them and that they enjoyed the diversity in the group. The fact there was space to hear one another's differences and not to have to toe a party line was very important. Here it was OK to simply 'be who you are'.

As Jenny left, she felt that this was a very warm and relational group, which was providing not only support and encouragement for each other on their respective Christian journeys, but also a place of nourishment for one another. This is not a group striving to meet other people's expectations or trying to 'get it right'. They seemed settled in their faith and in their stance as a group outside the Church.

Jenny's description of this particular group is a snippet of a small study of post-church groups. These groups were, typically, formed by people who, having left 'institutional' forms of church wanted to support and sustain each other in their spiritual journeys. Nearly all the respondents (well over 90 per cent) had left all forms of established Church prior to becoming involved in their post-church group and most (over 70 per cent) continued to have no involvement in any institutional Church. The connections the others had were typically marginal and sporadic. Perhaps the self-description of one of these groups sums up something of who they are:

> Many of our group have previously attended evangelical, Pentecostal or charismatic churches, but have moved on for a number of reasons, including a desire for more intimacy and honesty in relating with other Christians. In spite of this, we are not 'anti' the churches we have left, but simply feel they are not where we fit at present.

In many senses the *institutional* and *post-church* groups may be seen simply as different forms of Church. From a functional perspective institutional Churches and post-church groups may meet for similar purposes: to worship, to pray, to teach and be taught and to share the sacraments. What makes the post-church groups different isn't a theological or functional difference; rather, the differences are linked to culture and values. As one group member said:

> I haven't in effect left church. But my thinking has progressed beyond the church walls (so to speak) to the point where part of my Christian life can only be associated with a departure from the established Church.

Such groups not only *allow*, but actively *encourage* people to question, explore and search beyond the boundaries of discussions and teaching set down implicitly or explicitly in institutional forms of EPC church. The churches these people have left – which are predominantly conservative evangelical in theology and charismatic in style – are typically full of answers. The post-church groups these leavers form are in contrast focused on questions: exploration of questions, opening up of questions, looking behind 'answers' and challenging the 'known'. This was a common feature of all the groups we have encountered.

> *Jill* The group provides me with friendship – a place in which to grow spiritually. It is like being part of a family where I can relax a little and be me. It provides an environment of grace rather than law (I find this tends to bring out the best in a person). In contrast the traditional Church has tended (partly due to size, partly doctrine) to

encourage individualism and performance. This group rewards 'being' rather than 'doing' and is supportive even if you haven't succeeded in something.

While freedom to explore is important, belonging is also high on people's reasons for joining and remaining a part of these groups. A recurring theme is friendship. People repeatedly say that they continue to go to their group because they have close friends there who care for them, support them and whose company they enjoy. Clearly, there are very strong communities of care, friendship, accountability, humour and depth formed in these groups. But an equally common theme was 'safety'. Variations on the theme – 'The group provides a safe place where I can be myself' turned up time and again in people's comments. The issue of safety related to it being safe to grow spiritually; to participate, to be open, honest and real and to have vigorous, intelligent discussion and debate. As one woman put it, 'Our group is not precious.' Sarah sums up what such groups provide:

> *Sarah* I was looking for a place where I could be real. A place whose understanding of God and the spiritual journey allowed for reality. I was looking for a place where relationship was important and where it was acknowledged that there would be differences in the way we each outworked our spiritual journeys. A place where there was freedom for me to grow in the way I felt God was inviting me to. A place where I could support others and be supported by them.

These new post-church groups offer a number of hopeful possibilities for new ways of belonging. But like the institutional forms of Church, these groups too have their struggles. They are, typically, made up of a pretty homogeneous group of people representing a narrow strand of society. They are often educated, middle-class, middle-aged baby-boomers who tend to focus on faith and life issues affecting them or people like them. They typically struggle to provide adequately for the faith development of their children and teenagers. Although aware that this is an important priority, they find it difficult to meet the range of ages and needs. In fact this is the over-riding concern of people in post-church groups. In their 'flat leadership' (or no leadership) systems there is sometimes little sense of direction and for some members there is simply insufficient leadership.

Despite these limitations are these groups an indication of the future? I want to suggest that they are because we are moving through a major shift in culture, values and ways of understanding and operating in the world. Many writers have described the enormity of these shifts using the analogy of moving from dry land to being afloat in the ocean. Totally different rules apply between the two contexts, and the ways of operating in one context, for example on dry land, become completely inappropriate in the other, for example being afloat at sea. These are the metaphors used by sociologists David Lyon[3] and more extensively Zygmunt Bauman in their description of modern society as 'Liquid Modernity'[4] or liquid society. These metaphors help to see both how things are culturally changing and the extent of the changes that are occurring as we move from a 'modern' to a 'postmodern' world. Bauman explains the extent of the change by contrasting fluids that 'travel easily . . . flow, spill, run out, splash, pour, leak, flood, spray, drip, seep and ooze'[5] with solids which are fixed, dependable and stable. He argues that the solids of modernity are being liquefied not so they can be reformed into new solid structures but to remain perpetually in fluid motion under the new conditions of postmodernity. As this happens there is a loss of the old foundations: a loss of order, of structures and of systems. Living in this emerging 'liquid' world is metaphorically like leaving the dry land to travel at sea.[6] In this liquid world the Church is one of the structures – a solid – that is being liquefied.

Another leading sociologist, Manuel Castells, suggests that individuals, and organizations such as churches, have responded to this new environment in a number of different ways. The first is what he calls 'escapism' or the forming of a 'resistance identity'. Here people retreat from the insecurity and fluidity of the changing society into forms of fundamentalism where an external authority provides a foundation for knowledge, living and relationships. To use the analogy of liquids again, it means trying to sandbag a small piece of solid ground into an island.[7] As the waters are rising higher, more and more effort is needed for sandbagging the island. This escape response is based on two structures. First, the forming of a strong structural boundary between the outside world and the world of the resistance community which I have called sandbagging, and second a reliance on an external authority for what is seen as true and for making life and ethical decisions. The external authority can be a sacred text, special person or some other transcendent reference point. Whatever it is, the appeal is always to an external authority that is solid, authoritative, unquestioned and unquestionable. It is these kinds of churches which we see so many people leaving as they traverse their own dark nights and deserts of faith, forming as they do a much stronger reliance on an inner authority coupled with an openness and positive engagement of the wider society.

Castells' second possible response to the changing cultural climate is to do the exact opposite of the escapist response. It is simply that people embrace the chaos of the changes and go with the flow, as it were. Using the analogy this could mean diving off the dry land into the fluid world and simply going with its currents, tides, ebbs and flows. In this case authority is located in the individual who is freed of all anchor points to take and leave, follow and use all forms of knowledge, authority and experience to form their own sense of meaning and identity. Such individuals embrace the chaos of late modernity and in so doing find their meaning in the 'game', the exhilaration and the relativism of life itself. The idea is that in the world of 'Babel' you enjoy it for all it is worth and find your own pleasure and meaning along the way. Unlike the first escapist response, here there are clearly no boundaries and there is a free flow of experiences and information in this 'smorgasbord' approach to finding our own individual way.

In most discussions in Christian settings only these two options are identified. For in the black or white, right or wrong world of much Christianity it is suggested that either we have some external form of authority, a hierarchy of knowledge sources and clear boundaries, or we slip into relativism and personal choice. No other option is suggested. The problem is, neither option is particularly helpful in our social context. Parker Palmer notes that Augustine's advice, given some 1,500 years ago, seems to be still relevant today: 'Christians should neither identify themselves with the fortunes of the Empire (the wider culture), nor retreat into a defensive ghetto.' Like him, we must find another way because:

> The great things disappear in the face of both absolutism and relativism. With absolutism, we claim to know precisely the nature of great things, so there is no need to continue in dialogue with them – or with each other. The experts possess

the facts, and all that remains is for them to transmit those facts to those who do not know. With relativism, we claim that knowledge depends wholly on where one stands, so we cannot know anything with any certainty beyond our personal point of view. Once again, there is no need to continue in dialogue with great things or with each other: one truth for you, another for me, and never mind the difference.[8]

The third option Castells calls 'project identity' which involves an increasing engagement within the emerging culture in the process of 'becoming' rather than having arrived. This project of becoming can be seen, I want to suggest, as being part of a conversation in which personal identity and truth are found and shaped in conversation with personal experiences, sacred text and others. It is a form of narrative theology where my story is validated and linked with the stories of others, Christians of history and the stories of biblical characters. Here, in contrast to both of the preceding options, the subject, in our case what it means to be a Christ follower, is the focus of attention. Authority is located in the knower, the community of knowers and the subject of conversation. Identity is formed as the subject becomes better understood, and this knowledge shapes the person's life in convictional engagement with others and society at large. In this sense it is an identity based on a lived trust more than a cognitive belief.

What the sociologists are pointing to here is linked to what we discussed earlier in terms of truth and myth, because looking at the scriptures and Christianity through the lens of *myth* as understood by Tolkien, Lewis and Campbell, as conveyors of profound and essential truth, leads us to the place of *mysticism* and *mystics*. One of the early sociologists to write about the Church was Ernst Troeltsch. Put simply, he said that Christianity could be found in three basic forms. First there was the 'sect' in which adherents reject the surrounding society for the alternative teachings and culture of their sect. These sects normally have a culture of rigor, perfectionism and transformation. To use Jesus' words, in sects 'Those who are not for me are against me.' Troeltsch's second form of Christianity is the 'Church' which is more widely embracing and selectively open to the values of the wider society. The 'Church' is also much broader than the sect in who it can accommodate. In the 'Church' an ethos of 'Those who are not against me are for me' tends to be operative. His final form of Christianity he called 'mysticism'. 'The 'mystic' is primarily a subjective religious person who is not linked to any religious body or if one is linked one does not find it very important.'[9] 'The church emphasizes the sacraments and education; the sect emphasizes conversion and commitment; the mystic emphasizes inner experience.'[10]

The project identity described by Castells connects with the post-critical faith of Ricoeur, the later stages of faith described by Fowler, the faith of the desert and the faith that has endured the dark night described by St John of the Cross. Such a faith is marked, Alan Jones would claim, by a divided mind that, once acknowledged, is able to hold multiple perspectives and realities, an uneasy conscience that knows from first-hand experience that evil passes through us all and a lived sense of personal failure.[11] To these qualities I would want to add a deep compassion similar to that evidenced by Job after his encounter with God, by Ricoeur after his own encounter with suffering and evil, and Peter after John 21. It is my belief that the people who have these qualities of faith will be critical for the future hope of the world, Christianity and the Church. For these believers are rarely, if ever, zealots, fundamentalists or persecutors, while many go on to become the mystics, saints and statespeople of their respective communities.

A project identity can only be shaped in conversation with others and with previous followers. Therefore community in some form is essential for the continuing formation of this kind of faith. It is an unending project that is always in conversation with others.

When I went back to the church leavers I interviewed five years ago and asked them about their faith over the last five-plus years, there was a significant influence of faith groups in people's individual faith journeys. Of those who went on to develop a stronger and more definite Christian faith the vast majority were part of such groups.

Although *A Churchless Faith* suggested that these groups were highly influential on individuals' personal faith trajectories, a causative effect could not then be shown. This subsequent study which shows how people have moved in their faith over a five-year period now clearly indicates a relationship between a faith group involvement outside the institutional Church and people making moves towards a clearer, personally stronger and more definitive Christian faith. This indicates that much can be gained by individuals in the deconstruction and reconstruction of their faith if they are actively part of such a group; that is, groups where diversity, ambiguity, creative conflict, honesty and humility are encouraged. Here, there is a realization of the multiple nature of truth, and its inherent paradoxes are appreciated. At the same time it is recognized that truth may be conveyed through different forms – not only rationality, but also liturgy, story, poetry, art and music. For, as Michael Polanyi has said, 'We know reality only by being in community with it.'[12] Because this is so essential I want to underline it by drawing on the work of the anthropologist George Herbert Mead: 'There is no selfhood apart from community. The self is dependent upon the faithful response of others in community in order to form a reliable sense of identity, to shape its dominant interpretative image of the real and to develop conscience and conceptions of moral value.'[13]

A Churchless Faith ended by describing the faith journeys of people who could be described as 'wayfarers': those who are exploring ways forward as Christians in a new context. As we draw these chapters to a conclusion I want to focus less on the individual faith of those exploring beyond the boundaries and more on the forming of 'waystations': places where individual explorers can find and form communities that can provide deep wells for finding truth, forming identity, encouraging spiritual desire and engaging a changing world. The relationship between 'wayfarers' (*people* seeking to form a culturally relevant Christian faith within 'postmodern culture') and 'waystations' (*places* that foster, fund and develop such a faith) is hopefully obvious.

'Waystations' sponsor individuals to take seriously their own faith stories and the stories of the Christian and biblical tradition in the context of postmodern life. These are the kind of groups who have supported many of the people I have met as they move to a faith which they would personally characterize as 'clearer, stronger and more definitive'. The research is clear that, for those who describe their Christian faith in this way, participation in a faith group was almost universal.

A thousand years ago the Christian faith in the West was shaped by the building of cathedrals. In a similar way today the future of faith in the West may, at least partly, be determined by these postchurch groups: the new waystations. Forming such waystations is a far more modest endeavour compared to building a cathedral, but in a world where the old fixities of space and time have been broken down, we need communities of faith that will transcend space and time. Such communities will quite possibly be short-term, ever fluid and changing, and may even be continued across great distances of space, utilizing the convenience and speed of modern communications. In this way they will not be like the cathedrals of a previous era. In a fast-food culture dominated by microwave cooking and instant communication media the forms of Christian community that will be increasingly required are those that are themselves able to cross spatial locations and be far more 'of the moment'. The waystation provides a place for the individual to find meaning, develop identity, form friendships and care for others without jeopardizing their individuality. The waystation community life calls the individual to reconsider his or her life at all levels by his or her encounter with an alternative reality experienced in the waystation.[14]

I would like to lay out a dream for waystations of the future, suggesting that they be places where all are welcomed equally to join conversations about truth and God, where spiritual desire is encouraged while spiritual depth is modelled, and engagement with the needs and care of people is happening. The waystation will need to be made up of both transitory wayfarers who will come and go and others who will be committed to the waystation as its core of energy givers. Specifically waystations will, I suggest, include the following criteria. The points below are an ideal, a dream. Each gathering of people in search of Christian truth in the new cultural context will find its own evolving way, nevertheless these points may be helpful for group discussion.

1   The waystation is or has a place. It is something people can visit, albeit that they may visit through the Internet. In this sense waystations are not hidden.
2   All are welcomed to conversations about truth and God. The experience of everyone who visits the waystation is valued and listened to. Here it is accepted that all knowing is relative, partial and inevitably a distortion. Therefore the perspective of the outsider is welcomed as part of the conversation, while the subject – God – remains central.
3   The conversation(s) about truth, God and God's leading involve open conversations with those present, their experiences and

beliefs, sacred texts and previous followers of Christ in other eras. While all opinions and beliefs are valued, nevertheless at times those gathered will need to make corporate statements about truth, God and God's leading for them.

4 The committed core of the waystation model a depth of spirituality through shared liturgy, prayer and worship. This is the heart of the waystation itself; for the waystation is a well-digging community, and the well they are digging is into the depths of God.

5 The waystation needs tangible ways of meeting the needs of people in their small piece of the planet. This involves the care of the 'poor and needy'. These are the 'mission projects' of the waystation. Travellers are invited to join in the mission projects of the waystation while they are there.

6 Wayfarers will come and go. Some will come for a few hours, others for weeks or months, and some even for longer. Some will want to move from being visitors to being committed to the community. This means making very deep commitments, commitments that express the core beliefs, values and lifestyle of Christ.

This is the hope that Brenda carries for the future of the Church when she says:

> *Brenda* Church can be a place where people are empowered to be their true selves in all their fullness through God, to be the person of Jesus to their communities outside of church and be encouraged to become connected to the Source in a deeper more intimate way. Church can be a place that models life-giving community, that models Christ-like attitudes and decisions for living – a place that serves to draw people to God through Christ, because of the way we love God and each other.

We end with belonging and waystations because the journey into the dark night or the desert places of faith is not only about us as individuals. Increasingly we are seeing that the Church in the West is entering a dark night, a new exile, a desert journey as well. The settled period of Christendom is crumbling and with it the structures and ways of Church and the forms of faith that the Christendom model of Church has espoused. In this time the journeys of individual wayfarers and waystations become models for the future. They can be models of hope. Here I have suggested that our Christian faith can go through times of serious deconstruction, doubt, critique and darkness. In so doing ground is cleared, space is made and a gap is formed in which God can do a new thing. This is a second calling that is both linked to and distinctly different from our first calling.

I want to end by suggesting that this process of deconstruction and death of the old lays the space for God's bringing of new life and shape to the churches as well. For in and beyond the deserts of criticism, despair and doubt lies the possibility of a new call for corporate forms of Christian faith intimately linked to our individual calls to a post-critical naïvety.

Conclusion

———◁○▷———

The soul would have no rainbow had the eyes no tears.
(J. V. Cheney)[1]

I have been writing through three days of a cold southerly storm, and now as we reach the end through the window a rainbow has appeared against the dark, rain-soaked clouds. Arching in a perfect curve, unbroken, each band of colour is so clearly seen. At the same time the rain bangs on the window as the howling wind drives it almost horizontally at our house. To my right the base of the rainbow meets the airport runway in the valley below. Each plane that lands reflects the individual bands of colour as they pass through their broad grasp. A beautiful but momentary scene. Now, having typed these few sentences, the rainbow is gone, replaced by a small patch of blue sky which is opening in the dark clouds above. It is my hope that these pages convey something of a rainbow in the storm, the hope of an authentic integrated faith in Christ in and beyond the dark nights and deserts you now walk.

For some years I was part of a small group of four that met fortnightly early on a Tuesday morning at McDonald's to talk about our lives, faith, challenges and work. One of the men in the group subsequently moved to another city and has gone through his own desert experience of faith. Recently he wrote an article about his journey in a magazine. One section of his story seems a particularly poignant way to end:

> This year I have felt something begin to change within me. It is intangible and unfinished and non-engineered. I feel like I am on a return journey [he had previously spoken of his sense of journeying away from his former ways of faith], the destination

of which is as yet unknown. It is a journey marked by some road-signs.

Possibly I have turned a corner for a range of reasons. One has been the help I have received through spiritual direction. I have had a listening ear, which has been non-judgemental and which has given me some tools for assessing both the past and the present. This, along with more than the usual dollop of discretionary time, has helped me to gain some perspective on my disaffection, on the phenomenon of mid-life, and on my entire journey with God and others thus far. At the same time I am coming to terms with my questions about the reality and existence of God.

At an indefinable point in time I have somehow been able to make the simple decision again that God is real (don't ask me how), and that if the journey thus far has been legitimate, then it makes sense to see where it will now lead. This is not necessarily a rational decision, but simply a right one – a bit like Frodo's decision to venture into the dark lands of Mordor with the ring (*Lord of the Rings* scene).

I still waver at times between belief and disbelief, but at the same time I have a deep-seated impression that I am simply and fundamentally in need of God. What is reassuring is that this return journey is one that I am working out with God. It is not the result of methods prescribed for me by the latest Christian self-help manual.[2]

Notes

————◄◦►————

Preface

1 J. R. R. Tolkien, *Lord of the Rings* (HarperCollins, 1995), p. 167.

Chapter 1 Finding Our Way

1 Psalm 84.5 (NIV).
2 Here 'mainline' is taken to be one of the traditional denomina-
  tions, for example Anglican, Methodist, Presbyterian, Baptist etc.
3 Alan Jamieson, *A Churchless Faith: Faith Journeys Beyond the
  Churches* (London, SPCK, 2002).
4 Mary Tuomi Hammond, 'Restoring a damaged faith' (*The Other
  Side*, May/June 2000).
5 See Luke 15.4.
6 Philip Richter and Leslie J. Francis, *Gone But Not Forgotten:
  Church Leaving and Returning* (London, Darton, Longman and
  Todd, 1998), p. 146.
7 Paul Ricoeur, *The Symbolism of Evil* (New York, Harper & Row,
  1967), p. 349.
8 Jeremiah 1.10.
9 The award was conferred by Pope John Paul II on Paul Ricoeur in
  person on 6 July 2003 in Vatican City. See www.nd.edu/~ndethics/
  Ethics_news/news_copies/Paul_Ricoeur.htm
10 Walter Brueggemann, *Cadences of Home: Preaching Among
  Exiles* (Louisville, KY, Westminster John Knox Press, 1997), p. 3.

Chapter 2 Thriving In and Beyond the Desert

1 Deuteronomy 32.10 (NIV).
2 Isaiah 49.14–15.
3 Job 23.1–3 (GNB).
4 1 Samuel 20.1.
5 Job 7.20.

6 Psalm 88.

7 Philip Yancey, *Soul Survivor: How my Faith Survived the Church* (London, Hodder and Stoughton, 2001), pp. 202–3.

8 Psalm 89.46.

9 Psalm 62.1–2 (RSV).

10 Doug Reichel, 'Thoughts on the Desert Walk' (*Stimulus* 2:1, February 1994), pp. 11–16.

11 Reichel, 'Thoughts on the Desert Walk', p. 13.

12 Reichel, 'Thoughts on the Desert Walk', p. 15.

13 Deuteronomy 32.10 (NIV).

14 Isaiah 45.3 (NIV).

15 Reichel, 'Thoughts on the Desert Walk', p. 16.

16 Thomas H. Green, *Drinking from a Dry Well* (Notre Dame, IN, Ave Maria Press, 1991), pp. 26–7.

Chapter 3 Seeing In and Beyond the Dark

1 Job 29.1–3 (CEV).

2 Romans 5.2–5 (GNB).

3 Ricoeur, *The Symbolism of Evil*, p. 349.

4 George G. Hunter III, *The Celtic Way of Evangelism: How Christianity can Reach the West . . . Again* (Nashville, TN, Abingdon Press, 2000), p. 74.

5 Ecclesiastes 1.2 (GNB).

6 Huston Smith, *Why Religion Matters: The Fate of the Human Spirit in an Age of Disbelief* (New York, Harper & Row, 2001), p. 148.

7 1 Corinthians 15.19 (GNB).

8 John 6.68–69 (CEV).

9 John 1.14 (GNB).

10 John 1.5 (GNB).

11 Mike Riddell, *Godzone: A Traveller's Guide* (Oxford, Lion, 1992), p. 43.

12 Quoted in Iain Matthew, *The Impact of God: Soundings from St John of the Cross* (London, Hodder and Stoughton, 1995), pp. 54–5.

13 Matthew, *The Impact of God*, p. 11.

14 Matthew, *The Impact of God*, p. 16.

15 Isaiah 50.11 (TLB).

16 Thomas H. Green, *When the Well Runs Dry: Prayer Beyond the Beginnings* (Notre Dame, IN, Ave Maria Press, 1998), p. 139.

17 Used with the permission of the Revd Dr George Armstrong.

Chapter 4 Questions In and Beyond Answers

1 Rainer Maria Rilke, *Letters to a Young Poet* (New York, W. W. Norton & Co., 1993), p. 35.
2 Mary Tuomi Hammond, 'Restoring a damaged faith' (*The Other Side*, May/June 2000).
3 John 20.25 (GNB).
4 Job 30.20–24 (GNB).
5 Job 38.2–4 (GNB).
6 John 20.27 (GNB).
7 James W. Fowler and Sam Keen, *Life Maps: Conversations on the Journey of Faith*, ed. J. Berryman (Waco, TX, Word Books, 1985), p. 79.
8 T. A. Veling, *Living in the Margins: Intentional Communities and the Art of Interpretation* (New York, Crossroad, 1996), p. 145.
9 Hannah Ward and Jennifer Wild, *Guard the Chaos: Finding Meaning in Change* (London, Darton, Longman & Todd, 1995), p. 10.
10 Kathleen Norris, *Amazing Grace: Vocabulary of Faith* (New York, Riverhead, 1998), p. 299.
11 *Dominion Post*, 1 March 2003.
12 Lynne Reid Banks, quoted in Dorothy Millar, *Seeds for the Morrow: Inspiring Thoughts from Many Sources* (unpublished).
13 Lloyd Geering, *Christianity Without God* (Wellington, NZ, Bridget Williams, 2002), p. 84.
14 Parker J. Palmer, *The Courage to Teach: Exploring the Inner Landscape of a Teacher's Life* (San Francisco, Jossey-Bass, 1998), p. 62.
15 Palmer, *The Courage to Teach*, p. 65.
16 Palmer, *The Courage to Teach*, p. 55.
17 C. S. Lewis, *Prince Caspian* (London, Diamond Books/HarperCollins, 1997) chapter 10.
18 St John of the Cross, *The Ascent of Carmel*, Book One, 13.11.

Chapter 5 Truth In and Beyond Myth

1 Eric Fromm, *Escape from Freedom* (New York, Holt, Rinehart & Winston, 1963), pp. 74ff., quoted in Mansell Pattison, *Pastor and Parish: A Systems Approach* (Philadelphia, Fortress Press, 1977), p. 41.
2 Mary Tuomi Hammond, 'Restoring a damaged faith' (*The Other Side*, May/June 2000), p. 41.
3 Fromm, *Escape from Freedom*, p. 41.

4 Alan Jones, *Soul Making: The Desert Way of Spirituality* (San Francisco, HarperCollins, 1989), p. 7.
5 Michael White, *Tolkien: A Biography* (London, Little, Brown & Co., 2001), p. 135.
6 White, *Tolkien: A Biography*, p. 136.
7 White, *Tolkien: A Biography*, p. 136.
8 White, *Tolkien: A Biography*, p. 136.
9 White, *Tolkien: A Biography*, p. 136.
10 White, *Tolkien: A Biography*, pp. 136–7.
11 Andrew B. Newberg and others, *Why God Won't Go Away: Brain Science and the Biology of Belief* (New York, Ballantine Books, 2001), p. 56.
12 Newberg, *Why God Won't Go Away*, p. 56.
13 Quoted in Richard Holloway, *Dancing on the Edge: Faith in a Post-Christian Age* (London, HarperCollins, 1997), p. 51.

Chapter 6 Prayer In and Beyond Words

1 See <www.cpinternet.com/-ennyman/Mother-T.html>
2 Quoted in James Houston, *Prayer: Transforming Friendship* (Oxford, Lion, 1993), p. 6.
3 Houston, *Prayer: Transforming Friendship*, pp. 13–14.
4 Luke 7.45.
5 For example Romans 16.16; 1 Corinthians 16.20; 1 Thessalonians 5.26.
6 Psalm 22.1–2 (CEV).
7 Psalm 88.1.
8 C. S. Lewis, *The Lion, The Witch and the Wardrobe* (London, HarperCollins, 1997), p. 75.
9 Iain Matthew, *The Impact of God: Soundings from St John of the Cross* (London, Hodder and Stoughton, 1995), p. 57.
10 Matthew, *The Impact of God*, p. 61.
11 Matthew, *The Impact of God*, p. 64.
12 Roman Liturgy, Rite of Holy Week, Easter Vigil.
13 Marjorie Flower OCD, *The Poems of St John of the Cross* (Varroville, NSW, Australia).
14 Jean Pierre de Caussade, *The Sacrament of the Present Moment*.

Chapter 7 Alleluia In and beyond Agony and Absence

1 Nicholas Wolterstorff, *Lament for a Son* (London, SPCK, 1997), p. 81. Reproduced by permission of SPCK and Wm B. Eerdmans Publishing Co.
2 C. S. Lewis, *A Grief Observed* (San Francisco, HarperSanFrancisco, 1994), p. 41.

3 Annie Dillard, *Holy the Firm* (New York, Harper & Row, 1977), pp. 41–2.
4 Dillard, *Holy the Firm*, p. 47.
5 Mark 15.39.
6 Hebrews 5.8 (NIV).
7 Dietrich Bonhoeffer, *Letters and Papers from Prison* (London, SCM Press, 1971), p. 361.
8 Poem by the Revd Edward Shillito (1872–1948).
9 Wolterstorff, *Lament for a Son*.
10 Job 19.25–26 (AV).
11 Job 19.27 (CEV).

Chapter 8 Growth and Grace In and Beyond Failure
1 Job 14.7–9 (NIV).
2 1 Corinthians 15.8–11.
3 1 Corinthians 5.1 (GNB).
4 James 2.23 describes Abraham as the 'friend of God'.
5 David is described as having a heart after God (1 Kings 11.4).
6 Quoted in J. W. Fowler and R. W. Lovin, *Trajectories in Faith: Five Life Stories* (Nashville, TN, Abingdon Press, 1980), p. 164.
7 Fowler and Lovin, *Trajectories in Faith*, p. 164.
8 'Discipleship, Development and Pain', from *The Bridge*, No. 9, January 1995, pp. 26–7.
9 Romans 8.28 (NIV).
10 Richard Holloway, *Dancing on the Edge: Faith in a Post-Christian Age* (London, HarperCollins, 1997), p. 58.
11 John 21.15–19.
12 John 13.37.
13 John 13.38.
14 'Jesus replied, "You do not realise now what I am doing, but later you will understand."' (John 13.7 (NIV)).
15 John 18:15–18, 25–27.
16 'Jesus was walking beside the Sea of Galilee' (Matthew 4.18); 'Jesus appeared again to his disciples, by the Sea of Tiberias' (John 21.2; (NIV) footnote states 'That is, Sea of Galilee').
17 John 21.6.
18 John 21.12 (NIV).
19 John 1.42.
20 Luke 22.62 (NIV).
21 Tim Dearborn, *Beyond Confusion: the Ethic of Grace in a World of Works* (Seattle Pacific University PhD thesis, 1999), p. 4.
22 Definition of forgiveness used by the International Forgiveness Institute.

23 John 21.17 (NIV).
24 John 21.22 (NIV).
25 1 Peter 2.3 (GNB).
26 2 Corinthians 12.9 (CEV).
27 2 Corinthians 12.10 (NIV).
28 Quoted in Thomas H. Green, *Drinking from a Dry Well* (Notre Dame, IN, Ave Maria Press, 1991), p. 44.
29 Green, *Drinking from a Dry Well*, p. 44.
30 Green, *Drinking from a Dry Well*, p. 45.
31 Green, *Drinking from a Dry Well*, p. 45.
32 James 5.16.

Chapter 9 Trust In and Beyond Suspicion
1 Luke 24.13–25.
2 Luke 24.21 (GNB).
3 Luke 24.25–6 (GNB).
4 Luke 24.32 (NIV).
5 Luke 24. 33 (author's free paraphrase).
6 *Deconverts from Fundamentalist New Religious Groups in the Federal Republic of Germany and the United States: Biographical Trajectories, Transformation Processes and the Need for Intervention: Exposé of Research*. Prof. Heinz Streib (2002).
7 Hannah Hurnard, *Hinds' Feet on High Places* (Wheaton, IL, Living Books, Tyndale House Publishers, 1993).
8 Philip Richter and Leslie Francis, *Gone But Not Forgotten* (London, Darton, Longman and Todd, 1998), p. 53.
9 Sharon Parks, *The Critical Years: The Young Adults Search for a Faith to Live By* (San Francisco, Harper & Row, 1986), p. 24.
10 Alan Jones, *Soul Making: The Desert Way of Spirituality* (San Francisco, HarperCollins, 1989), p. 22.
11 The titles used for each stage are taken from Charles R. McCollough, *Heads of Heaven, Feet of Clay* (New York, Pilgrim Press, 1983). Fowler's titles for each stage are: Stage 1 Intuitive-projective; Stage 2 Mythical-literal; Stage 3 Synthetic-conventional; Stage 4 Individuative-reflective; Stage 5 Conjunctive; Stage 6 Universalizing.
12 James W. Fowler, *Stages of Faith: The Psychology of Human Development and the Quest for Meaning* (HarperSan Francisco, 1995), pp. 122–34.
13 M. Scott Peck, *Further Along the Road Less Traveled: The Unending Journey Toward Spiritual Growth* (New York, Simon & Schuster, 1993), p. 121.

14 Fowler, *Stages of Faith*, p. 173.
15 Jack R. Pressau, *I'm Saved, You're Saved – Maybe* (Atlanta, GA, John Knox Press, 1977).
16 James W. Fowler, *Faith Development and Pastoral Care* (Philadelphia, Fortress Press, 1987), p. 91.
17 Fowler, *Faith Development and Pastoral Care*, p. 93.
18 James W. Fowler, *Becoming an Adult, Becoming Christian: Adult Development and Christian Faith* (San Francisco, Harper & Row, 1984), p. 65.
19 Fowler, *Becoming an Adult, Becoming Christian*, p. 65.
20 Fowler, *Becoming an Adult, Becoming Christian*, p. 65.
21 James Fowler and Sam Keen, *Life Maps: Conversations on the Journey of Faith*, ed. J. Berryman (Waco, TX, Word Books, 1985), p.81.
22 Fowler, *Becoming an Adult, Becoming Christian*, p. 65.
23 Fowler, *Becoming an Adult, Becoming Christian*, pp. 65–6.
24 Fowler, *Becoming an Adult, Becoming Christian*, p. 67.
25 Luke 22.42 (RSV).
26 Fowler, *Stages of Faith*, p. 294.
27 Job 3.11 (NIV).
28 Job 10.3 (NIV).
29 Job 13.23–24 (NIV).
30 Job 12.13 (NIV).
31 Job 16.19 (NIV).
32 Job 13.15 (AV).
33 Janet O. Hagberg and Robert A. Guelich, *The Critical Journey: Faith Journeys Beyond the Churches* (Dallas, TX, Word, 1989), p. 99.

Chapter 10 The Gospel In and Beyond Evangelism

1 'Bothering with God' (*Dominion Post*, 19 April 2003), p. F4.
2 Matthew 13.24–30.
3 Matthew 25.31–33.
4 Matthew 7.21.
5 Matthew 21.31.
6 Matthew 18.3.
7 Matthew 15.28.
8 Alan Jones, *Soul Making: The Desert Way of Spirituality* (San Francisco, HarperCollins, 1989), p. 9.
9 Jones, *Soul Making*, p. 11.
10 Jones, *Soul Making*, p. 172.

11 Paul Hawker, *Soul Survivor: A Spiritual Quest Through 40 Days and 40 Nights of Mountain Solitude* (British Columbia, Northstone, 1999).
12 Paul Hawker, *Secret Affairs of the Soul: Ordinary People's Extraordinary Experiences of the Sacred* (British Columbia, Northstone, 2000).
13 Matthew 11.25 is an example.
14 Hans Küng, *The Catholic Church: A Short History* (London, Weidenfeld & Nicolson, 2001), p. 113.
15 Matthew 9.22 (CEV).
16 Matthew 18.3 (CEV).
17 Hawker, *Secret Affairs of the Soul*, p. 176.
18 Matthew 10.8 (CEV).
19 Sheila Pritchard, 'Wells and Fences: the Risk of Spiritual Growth' (*Stimulus*, Vol. 7. No. 4, 1999), pp. 25–6.
20 Acts 17.22–3 (CEV).

Chapter 11 Commitment to People and the World In and Beyond Mission

1 Quoted from Dorothy Millar, *Seeds for the Morrow: Inspiring Thoughts from Many Sources* (unpublished) and Peter Millar, *Finding Hope Again: Journeying Through Sorrow and Beyond* (London, SCM-Canterbury Press, 2003), p. 166.
2 John 21.1 – some versions say 'Sea of Tiberias', named after the Emperor; often footnotes gloss this as the Sea of Galilee.
3 Matthew 4.18.
4 John 18.18.
5 John 13.7.
6 John 21.17.
7 Jeremiah 12.5 (NIV).
8 Paul Ricoeur, *The Symbolism of Evil* (New York, Harper & Row, 1967), p. 321.
9 Job 42.5 (NIV).
10 Job 40.4.
11 John 21.19.
12 Genesis 15.
13 Genesis 15.5.
14 Micah 6.8 (NIV).
15 Hasidic tale quoted in Dorothy Millar, *Seeds for the Morrow: Inspiring Thoughts from Many Sources* (unpublished booklet).
16 Interfaith Council for Peace and Justice, quoted in Peter Millar, *Finding Hope Again: Journeying Through Sorrow and Beyond* (London, SCM-Canterbury Press, 2003), p. 192.

Chapter 12 Belonging In and Beyond the Church

1 Quoted in Peter Millar, *Finding Hope Again: Journeying Through Sorrow and Beyond* (London, SCM-Canterbury Press, 2003), p. 184.

2 A drink made by spooning ice cream into the bottom of a glass and topping up with fizzy lemonade.

3 David Lyon, *Postmodernity* (Milton Keynes, Open University Press 1994), p. 11.

4 Zygmunt Bauman, *Liquid Modernity* (Cambridge, Polity Press, 2000).

5 Bauman, *Liquid Modernity*, p. 2.

6 Of course we constantly need to remind ourselves that we are not the first to face a changing and disorienting social context. Augustine wrote *The City of God* as the Roman Empire crumbled, arguing that Christians should neither identify themselves with the fortunes of the Empire nor retreat into a defensive ghetto (David Lyon, *Postmodernity* (Milton Keynes, Open University Press 1994), p. 84.

7 Manuel Castells, *The Power of Identity* (Oxford, Blackwell, 1997).

8 Parker J. Palmer, *The Courage to Teach: Exploring the Inner Landscape of a Teacher's Life* (San Francisco, Jossey-Bass, 1998), p. 109.

9 G. E. Paul, 'Why Troeltsch? Why Today?' (*Christian Century* 30 June–7 July 1993), p. 677.

10 Paul, 'Why Troeltsch? Why Today?', p. 677.

11 Alan Jones, *Soul Making: The Desert Way of Spirituality* (San Francisco, HarperCollins, 1989), pp. 117–23.

12 Cited in Palmer, *The Courage to Teach*, pp. 98–9.

13 Cited in James Fowler, *To See the Kingdom: The Theological Vision of H. Richard Niebuhr* (Eugene, OR, Wipf and Stock; previously published by Abingdon Press, TN, 1994).

14 These responses have connections with three of the stages of faith. Escapism can be linked to Stage Three's tribalism and conformity, Stage Four's individuation to the embracing of cultural reality and Stage Five's balance of individualism and community, paradoxical ways of knowing and embracing mysterious truth to an emerging engagement with the new cultural realities. Of the three ideal types presented, the last offers the most hope for Christian identity and community in 'postmodernity'.

Conclusion

1 J. V. Cheney, quoted in James Jones, *Why do People Suffer? The Scandal of Pain in God's World* (Oxford, Lion, 1993), p. 13.
2 Used with permission of *Reality* magazine (www.reality.org.nz).

Every effort has been made to trace the owners of copyright material. We apologize for any errors or omissions that may remain, and would ask those concerned to contact the publishers, who will ensure that full acknowledgement is made in the future.